ROUTLEDGE LIBRARY EDITIONS: LIBRARY AND INFORMATION SCIENCE

Volume 31

THE ELECTRONIC JOURNAL

THE ELECTRONIC JOURNAL
The Future of Serials-Based Information

Edited by
BRIAN COOK

Routledge
Taylor & Francis Group

LONDON AND NEW YORK

First published in 1992 by The Haworth Press, Inc.

This edition first published in 2020
by Routledge
2 Park Square, Milton Park, Abingdon, Oxon OX14 4RN
and by Routledge
52 Vanderbilt Avenue, New York, NY 10017

Routledge is an imprint of the Taylor & Francis Group, an informa business

© 1992 The Haworth Press, Inc.

All rights reserved. No part of this book may be reprinted or reproduced or utilised in any form or by any electronic, mechanical, or other means, now known or hereafter invented, including photocopying and recording, or in any information storage or retrieval system, without permission in writing from the publishers.

Trademark notice: Product or corporate names may be trademarks or registered trademarks, and are used only for identification and explanation without intent to infringe.

British Library Cataloguing in Publication Data
A catalogue record for this book is available from the British Library

ISBN: 978-0-367-34616-4 (Set)
ISBN: 978-0-429-34352-0 (Set) (ebk)
ISBN: 978-0-367-36216-4 (Volume 31) (hbk)
ISBN: 978-0-367-36217-1 (Volume 31) (pbk)
ISBN: 978-0-429-34463-3 (Volume 31) (ebk)

Publisher's Note
The publisher has gone to great lengths to ensure the quality of this reprint but points out that some imperfections in the original copies may be apparent.

Disclaimer
The publisher has made every effort to trace copyright holders and would welcome correspondence from those they have been unable to trace.

The Electronic Journal: The Future of Serials-Based Information

Brian Cook
Editor

The Haworth Press, Inc.
New York • London • Norwood (Australia)

The Electronic Journal: The Future of Serials-Based Information has also been published as *Australian & New Zealand Journal of Serials Librarianship*, Volume 3, Number 2 1992.

© 1992 by The Haworth Press, Inc. All rights reserved. No part of this work may be reproduced or utilized in any form or by any means, electronic or mechanical, including photocopying, microfilm and recording, or by any information storage and retrieval system, without permission in writing from the publisher. Printed in the United States of America.

The Haworth Press, Inc., 10 Alice Street, Binghamton, NY 13904-1580, USA

Library of Congress Cataloging-in-Publication Data

The Electronic journal : the future of serials-based information / Brian Cook, editor.
    p. cm.
  Includes bibliographical references.
  ISBN: 1-56024-452-6
    1. Libraries–Australia–Special collections–Electronic journals–Congresses. 2. Electronic journals–Australia–Congresses. I. Cook, B. (Brian)
Z692.S5E42 1993
026.0253'432–dc20   93-19969
                                                                                                CIP

The Electronic Journal: The Future of Serials-Based Information

CONTENTS

Introduction	1
The Electronic Journal: Is the Future with Us? *Jolanda L. von Hagen*	3
The Economics of Scholarly Information: A Dissolving Triangle? *Tom Cochrane*	17
Introduction	17
Economic Pressures	17
The Scholar	22
Electronic Communication as It Is now	24
Future Developments and The Role of the Stakeholders	26
Conclusion	28
When the Electronic Journal Comes to the Campus *Carol Newton-Smith*	31
What Is an Electronic Journal?	31
Electronic versus Paper Journal	31
Types of Electronic Journal	34
How to Find Out About Electronic Journals	36
What to Do with Them when They Arrive	38
Conclusion	43

Access to Journal Information and the Impact of New
Technologies 45
Anne H. Newell

The Queensland University of Technology Environment 46
Survey Methodology 48
Analysis of Survey Responses and Key Findings 50
In Summary, Where Does This Lead Us? 64

The E-Journal: Experiences at the State Library
of New South Wales 69
Janine Schmidt

The View from the Other Side of the Disc 79
Julie Stevens

Why Me? 79
ALDIS Pty Ltd 79
The Issue at Hand: Image Databases 80
Image Databases: How They Work 81
The Impact of the Issue 81
In Conclusion 86

Cyberspace Economics 89
Don Lamberton

The Electronic Journal: The Day in Retrospect 101
Brian Cook

The Papers 101
Threads That Emerged 104

Introduction

There is little need to remind readers that advances in the use of technology in libraries over the past decade or so have revolutionised the way clients view services offered. Expectations of electronic delivery are up and increasingly people enquire especially in the academic environment, about the next advance and "When can I have the information on my desk?"

The advent of the electronic journal, though slow, only adds to the plethora of information now available in electronic format directly to clients. As outlined or implied in Carol Newton-Smith's article, electronic journals will permit people to have easy access to information contained in articles, direct notification of availability, searching by a range of descriptions, use of Boolean logic to refine searching, use of a number of platforms for access and transfer of copies into personal systems. These advantages only cover some of the possibilities for the use of information that will be available in electronic journals given developments occurring in hardware and access software.

The papers contained in this volume are the products of a seminar run at Bond University in May, 1992 and sponsored by the Australian Serials Special Interest Group and the Australian Council of Libraries and Information Services. The title–The Electronic Journal: The Future of Serials-Based Information–captured the theme of the day which was about possibilities and realities with increased use of electronic means for the publication of scholarly literature.

In welcoming participants the Manager of Bond University Library, Sandra Jeffries, stated that at present the concept of the "e-journal . . . tends to raise more questions than answers and has implications for journal publishers, suppliers, librarians and their clients." As the seminar unfolded this proved to be a truism. Notwithstanding this, there is no doubt that the articles contained herein

© 1992 by The Haworth Press, Inc. All rights reserved.

went a long way to outlining the issues, to indicating trends, to setting challenges and to highlighting the need for libraries and their clients to become more familiar with what will, no doubt, be a growing trend.

The papers are presented as delivered at the seminar and no attempt has been made to edit them.

Brian Cook
Griffith University

The Electronic Journal: Is the Future with Us?

Jolanda L. von Hagen

Is the future with us—are journal articles written for and used through an electronic carrier a separate segment in the lives of scientists, publishers and librarians? If in present terms we continue on the path into the future, where will it lead to? Assuming all academic information is collected and disseminated only by electronic means are we professionally equipped to deal with it? What is the role of the author? Will he or she get unbiased peer review? Will they index, abstract and categorize their articles? How will the citation process work? Will they, the authors, get recognition for their labours? What is the role of the publisher and the librarian?

As a member of the community of international Scientific Technical and Medical—or STM—publishers, I am conscious of the danger that you might think I may have a crystal ball and know all the answers to these questions that concern us for the future. I assure you I know I don't, and I cannot even apologize for it.

Therefore, rather than give one single publisher's opinion, I have done what publishers do—I have selected, sorted, evaluated and collected relevant facts—you may challenge what I consider relevant—and tried to stay within the role publishers play. I will refer to statements and points made by distinguished professionals in the scientific, publishing and library community and apply my own interpretations. At times it is helpful to stop and step back to look at the situation from an overall perspective.

For me the most important question is what does the reader/user (many times the authors themselves) need/want; how do they need it and how can we best provide it. It is all one question. I will not go into technical developments, the program provides several points to do that later.

The nineties, which still are part of our future, have been troublesome in many ways. Science as a vital part of society and people's well-being is, if not threatened, at least questioned.

A statement made by the president of the American Association for the Advancement of Science at the end of last year reads:

> The nineties find science in a paradox. Never has its role been more critical to the health and well being of the world, yet never has its own standing been more in jeopardy. Scientific advances are the key to addressing nations' greatest crises but science funding and talent pools are now both threatened, more so through perception with the academic, but even wider-spread in the university and library communities, saying science and research findings should be kept within their own walls and made use of through their own networks.

The AAAS and many scientists/researchers as authors agree that the reality of these goals would limit access to information and counteract the role science is meant to fulfill in society.

Let us review the situation: where we come from, where we are and where–may be–the future will take us.

Many of us have been trying to make predictions about the electronic future for more than a decade and we have been wrong more often than right. I remember a meeting with European and American STM publishers and Russian scientists in 1979 where some publishers predicted that, by the end of the 1980s, academic journal articles would not be printed on paper any more (I might add that the Russian scientists shuddered at that thought, because they would be excluded from any publication). Today I would hesitate to make a serious prediction as to when most (and I would like to underline most) journals complete with graphics will be available in ASCII form. It might be 5 years or by the end of this century.

The errors in our predictions of a decade ago were in two major respects:

1. The timing of key events–that is, the point in time when full text and graphics of the majority of traditional journals would be available in a searchable on-line environment, and
2. in foreseeing the intervening developments which changed the market–meaning the library world.

The rapid expansion in networks used by faculty and students on and between campuses and by researchers in industry is the most dramatic change. The exhilarating discussions with NREN and the work done by CNI during the past two years have proven these predictions wrong on even more counts.

All this happened simultaneously with the acute problem in serials purchasing caused by currency fluctuations and troublesome world economies. Publishers observed the libraries' reactions: to look for ways to get more for the same or less. With local and academic networks available, it was natural to look for networked information delivery. The questions raised were–how can we make better use of the collections we own and how to decide on what to own and which to provide on demand–and photocopying increased!

What did (and what do) the publishers do?

I would like to reflect a little on how STM publishers view themselves as an industry. To quote Jon Baumgarten, Legal Counsel to the Association of American Publishers:

> To the contemporary STM publisher the work of individual authors is increasingly just the starting point in the publisher's own creative process of identification, selection, coordination and editing, the publisher's crafting of new information products and services, and the publisher's development of new systems for the efficient dissemination and use of scientific knowledge in a manner responsive to the needs of research. This is the function the consumer and individual author cannot fulfill.

or as eloquently expressed by Gordon Graham in a leaflet for the recent meeting of the International Publishers Association in New Delhi, India:

> Publishing today has changed in structure and method, but not in substance. It remains what it always has been–the art of

creative and effective communication, which is seminal to the democratic society. Most publishers today, contrary to popular belief, are still small, but publishing as a whole is big business, dramatised by about 2 dozen mega corporations, which describe themselves as the multi-media communications industry. The multi-mega phenomenon is effect not cause. What has transformed publishing is the information explosion, the development of technology to handle it and the consequent threat to the rights of authors and publishers.

By the 1990s publishers have by and large adjusted to the information society, although all maintain the same purpose–to be the catalyst between author and reader.

To stay in business they have to protect their right to publish, transferred to them by the author. Mari Pijnenborg of Elsevier has said it best:

> We are in the business of fast and tailormade dissemination of scientific information; protection of our rights is a tool not the target.

This applies to commercial as well as society publishers, with journals being more important to scientists and professionals as a publishing outlet and a quick source of current information.

I do not want to dwell on copyright. It is well known fact that in the 1980's publishers were severely damaged by photocopying. To avoid further economic and functional difficulties they adjusted their prices. They don't want to repeat this experience. Electronic publishing does require more effort, more investment and added value on the part of the publisher than print publishing and even more now than in the past they have to protect their rights. Authors rely on publishers to have their work protected. Contrary to the opinion expressed by some of your colleagues, authors do insist on having their intellectual property protected. For them copyright is not obsolete. This is neither the time nor the place to pursue copyright issues in the 90s. But I am always reminded of an article published in 1945 in the Columbia Law Review by Professor Chafee where he states:

> Copyright is the Cinderella of Law. Her rich older sisters, Franchises and Patents, long crowded her into the chimney corner. Suddenly the fairy godmother, invention, endowed her with mechanical and electrical devices as magical as the pumpkin coach and the mice footmen. Now she whirls through the mad mazes of the glamorous ball.

Nearly 50 years later the mad mazes seem to be as mad as ever.

Assuming that intellectual property can and will be protected in an electronic environment, let's look at where we are now. How do publishers respond to the pressure from the market to provide information cheaper and faster?

If we are talking about the literal electronic journal where everything including graphics is available in ASCII mode, publishers are responding slowly. One reason is that international journals cannot be switched from paper to electronic on any given day; manuscript preparation from scientists around the world varies widely. Another reason is economics. It requires large investments to prepare for electronic delivery.

Let us not forget that many STM publishers are small. They publish important contributions to science development. But they do not have the resources to prepare for electronic delivery. The large publishers are making huge investments. The technology is available. Many research centres and some publishers have their publications stored in digitized form; and indeed some electronic journals are on the market.

Yet publishers and librarians realise they have to provide both paper and electronics. Access to journals will have to be improved by making use of the networks to bring the journal's contents faster to the region. Networks, on-line, CD-ROM or floppy disk can be used, but that still does not solve the problem of making the information available as soon as it passes the peer review and is accepted by the editor of the journal.

These improvements will however reduce publication time. As we continue on this path almost all text will be in digital form at some point in the process of publication–this is not yet true for illustrations–but at present very few texts are published in digital form.

At present the changes which realistically provide faster delivery are "Current Awareness Services" and "Electronic Document Delivery." With few exceptions that means the electronic availability of the journal's table of contents at or just before publication of the issue. I venture to say for the majority of academic and research journals this will be the "electronic journal" for the next few years.

The opportunity for faster access to information with electronic media has not only been recognised by libraries and their local, national and international networks. They have been picked up by a number of players, such as industrial companies and subscription agents as well as indexing and bibliographic services. They all see a new business here. They want publisher's permission to electronically store (scanning the images from the printed journal), redistribute and in most cases sell, full text or individual article copies. The problem at this time is that most publishers do not know what to charge for the permission to store electronically or for the electronic copy.

Intermediary organisations including universities as well as publishers have invested huge amounts of money to develop new systems of access. The only real result the publishers have achieved is ADONIS. I know this will come up in the program later, therefore suffice it to say it took more than 10 years, lots of funds and agonizing over decisions to get where we are today. I know because I was involved in the project for Springer in the early 80s.

We know at present it is still a dream to do large scale full text with graphics on-line searching via networks. At the moment the scanning and storing could be called electronic access or even electronic publishing. From that, archives of electronically scanned journal articles, which are stored and retrieved on demand, will be built.

As was said earlier, will publishers–and to make it a viable information base it cannot only mean the mega corporations mentioned before–agree to uncontrolled exploitation and distribution of what they call their product, developed at high costs?

Systems are being developed or improved by organisations such as:

CARL Systems Inc.,
Faxon Research Service Center,
ISI–through Current Contents,
BIDS–Bath Information Data Systems,
Engineering Index,
UMI,
and ADONIS.

The model system would be a "Current Awareness System for Individual Article Supply" (to make it difficult there is already an acronym for it–CASIAS) with these elements:

a. Retrieval to lead to a document delivery system
b. Access to lead to a current alerting system
c. Distribution to lead to electronic networks
d. Delivery by hard copy via mail or fax
e. Workstations to be used via personal computers.

What are the users' expectations?

Price	-	US $ 10 to 15 per document?
Speed	-	24 hours?
Format	-	Printed
Accessibility	-	Ease of use
Comprehensiveness	-	Minimum 5,000 titles?

And what are the publishers/authors' expectations?

Copyright protection
Royalty payments direct or through agencies
Market feedback

The future of a CASIAS system technology could be:

Access	-	keyboarding, using standards like SGML
Retrieval	-	through Document Delivery Centers as identified earlier

Distribution   -   through INTERNET, BITNET, NREN, AARNET, JANET, SUPERJANET, etc.
Format   -   through hardcopy by mail, fax or screen print.

What would this system mean for the library community?

- Libraries will have to review their mission and goals and bring them in line with their institutions, i.e., university or corporation;
- they will have to focus on contents and delivery;
- they will have to supply knowledge not just information;
- their accountability will increase;
- they will be judged by their performance not their collection;
- they will have to be a "learning organisation" to satisfy the increased demands from the reader/user,

to follow what Ward Shaw of CARL says "through libraries to users."

Another scenario in this electronic use for dissemination could be that publishers would (and some do) experiment with scientists and article authors by sending the Table of Contents to their mail boxes. If implemented more widely, what effect would this change in distribution directly to the end user have on the library? If a library participated in such an experiment, should the service be restricted to the local network? Would the availability of such a service stimulate demand from faculty to purchase the journal or get full text document delivery? Would a library work with any or many publishers to create an electronic mail current awareness service only in reference to its collection? Again, the biggest obstacle still is that there are no pricing models for these transactions.

Where do we go from here?

Publishers must find faster, more cost effective ways for electronic use of their material and at the same time they must find ways to provide the services of disseminating the information on paper at acceptable prices. Both are tall orders. Librarians, however, would be very wise not to blame publishers for all their financial difficulties. Science itself has caused most of the changes highlighted by the lack of local and federal funds.

Publishers will continue to have a creative role in electronic publishing with the activity to select, combine, present and deliver digitised information from various sources. The presentation and delivery are considered very important. We see interesting developments in desk top publishing (lay-out), presentation systems, documentation systems, interactive systems and integrated systems (texts, stills, video and sound) as well as information management systems. Among the new developments are SGML, hypertexts, and multi-media. SGML (Standard Generalized Markup Language) is considered to be a tool for managing information for a variety of users. Hypertext is a higher level abstracting and navigation instrument in and between documents. Multi-media are the integrated hardware and software components providing access to a wide variety of types of documents in their own internal format including text, vector mode graphic images and diagrams. The publishing workflow is gradually changing in the areas of technical documentation and information; integrated publishing systems can and will eliminate various steps in the process (See Figures 1 and 2).

While I am troubled by many aspects of the changes in information dissemination, because we have not yet built the much needed close collaboration with all players involved, I am excited by the new role publishers and librarians can and, I am certain, will play. I could continue for a long time to toss ideas into the air and have them come back as questions. For the moment, however, I would like to conclude with a look at the range of new products which are now appearing (Figure 3).

I am sure more options for new products do exist. The question raised earlier remains—who will use them and how?

The electronic process, be it in business or in the academic environment, has a very high profile but when it comes to actual usage the profile is still very low. In looking at these possible new products I would like to borrow from a paper presented at a recent STM publishers meeting. Mr. Waaijers of the Delft University of Technology Library threw another large stone to make major ripples in the publishers' sea of thoughts and at the same time caused uneasiness among some of his colleagues in the audience simply by

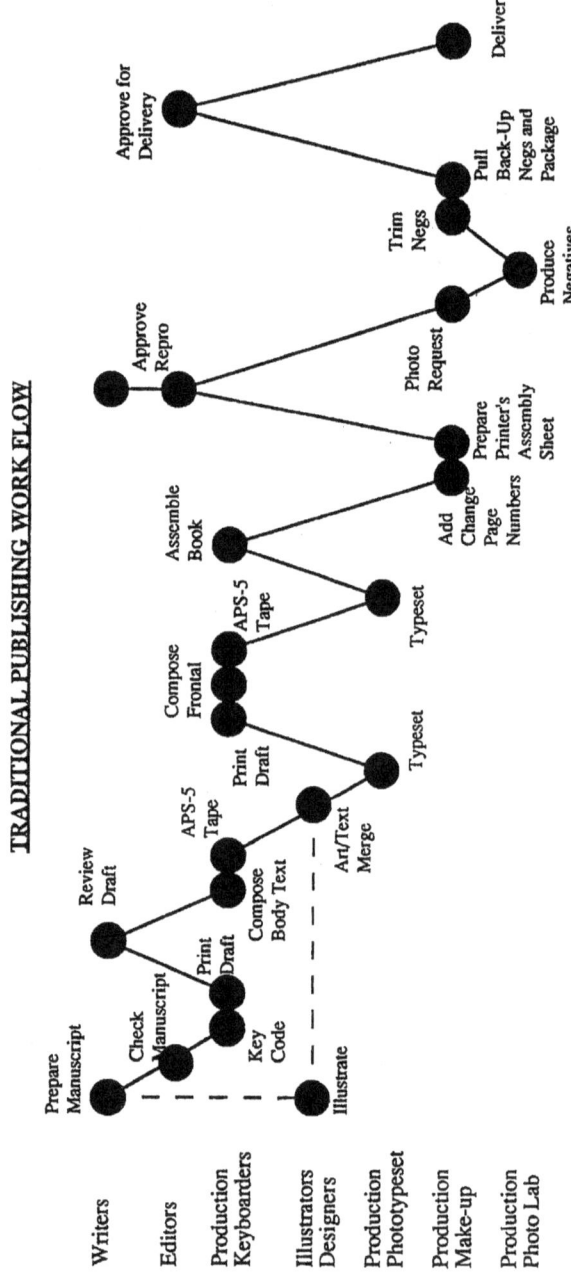

FIGURE 1
TRADITIONAL PUBLISHING WORK FLOW

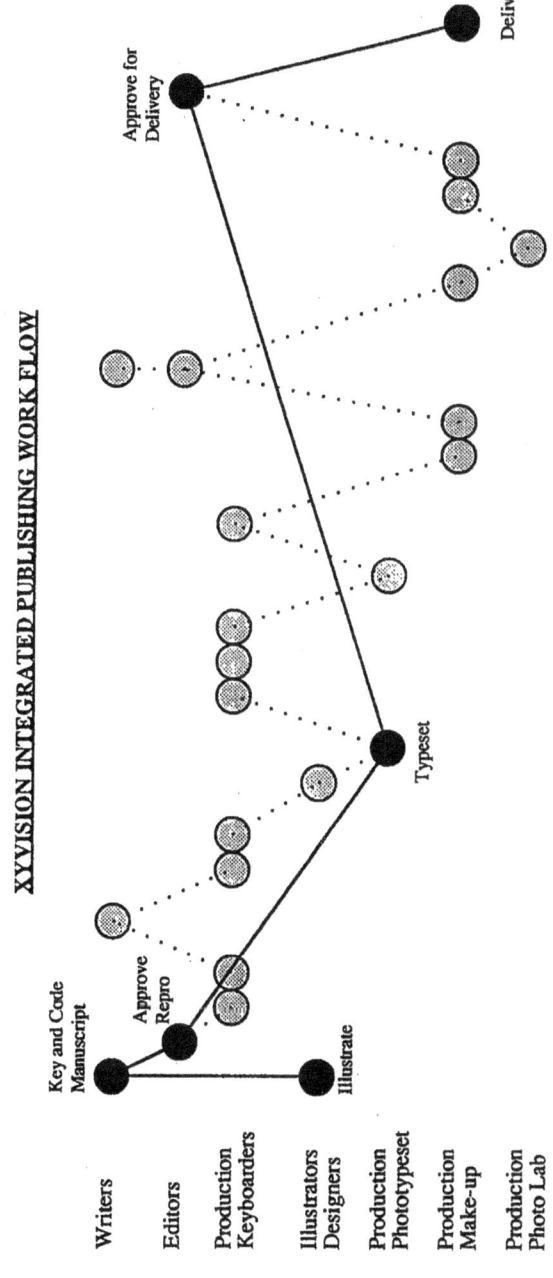

FIGURE 2

XYVISION INTEGRATED PUBLISHING WORK FLOW

FIGURE 3

A NEW FAMILY OF PRODUCTS:

OPTICAL DISKS

AUDIO CD	▶	CD–ROM CD–VIDEO CD-I DATAROM OROM MINI-CD-ROM WORM DRAW ERASABLE (MANY PATENTS PENDING)
LASER-VISION	▶	LV-ROM MEDIUM AND LARGE CAPACITY OPTICAL DISKS
LASER CARDS	▶	READ ONLY LASER CARD WRITE/READ LASER CARD
MEMORY CARDS	▶	READ ONLY MASK ROM CARD READ/WRITE EEPROM CARD REWRITABLE EPROM CARD

SOFTSTRIP SYSTEM

TDB (PAPER ROM)

asking from the librarians' point of view—"what does the evasive end user want?" He reviewed the possible new products and their characteristics as data carriers based on:

    a. accessibility
    b. timeliness
    c. compactness
    d. searchability

e. preservability
f. authenticity, and
g. appearance.

Figure 4 shows the comparisons he arrived at.

To quote Mr. Waaijers: "Since paper still essentially has pluses where its competitors have minuses, my conclusion is that it will be with us for quite some time to come. Further it is noteworthy that paper and on-line full text databases are fully complementary." Referring to authenticity he said: "As long as teenagers can hack a Pentagon computer and find top secret information on the deployment of tanks during a war in the Arabian desert, on-line databases are not the best safeguard to authenticity and intellectual property protection," and commenting on appearance he said: "I don't think you will impress your relatives very much by telling them that your brilliant thoughts are electronically stored somewhere in a computer together with hundreds of thousands of other brilliant thoughts. Since a publication is like a child to its author, the hardcopy edition is a child of flesh and blood. Its electronic counterpart is a child in the world of virtual reality."

Better than any device to date, the computer stores, manipulates, transforms, dispenses and distributes information, hence talented people in the industry are changing computers from simple tools for education into the educational process itself. We are a link in the

FIGURE 4

	PAPER	CD-ROM	ONLINE
Accessibility	+	−	−
Timeliness	−	−	+
Compactness	−	+	+
Searchability	−	+	+
Preservability	+	+	−
Authenticity	+	+	−
Appearance	+	−	−

information chain and as publishers and librarians, we certainly will need to collaborate to provide viable services now and in the future to the information society. If we accept that, today is already part of tomorrow and we will succeed.

The Economics of Scholarly Information: A Dissolving Triangle?

Tom Cochrane

INTRODUCTION

The triangle which is the topic of this discussion is the one which exists between the scholar, the publisher and the Library. There are other players who have roles in the interplay between these three. (Figure 1 Illustrates.) Editors, reviewers (including peer reviewers), and library suppliers obviously have positions somewhere in that triangle, but what I propose to do this afternoon is concentrate on the shape of that triangle, particularly the nexus between the three entities as it has developed to the present, and look at ways in which it is under challenge (or threat) as a consequence of new ways of doing things under the influence of technological innovation.

A lot of the most interesting literature on this subject emanates from North America. For us here in Australia, however, the social and economic structures involved in the concept of the political economy of scholarly publishing are quite similar. And because the data are so good for North America I am reliant on them to a considerable degree in this analysis.

ECONOMIC PRESSURES

Few here need reminding that one of the dominant issues in the management of academic libraries in Australia in the last few years has been the surging price of printed information, especially jour-

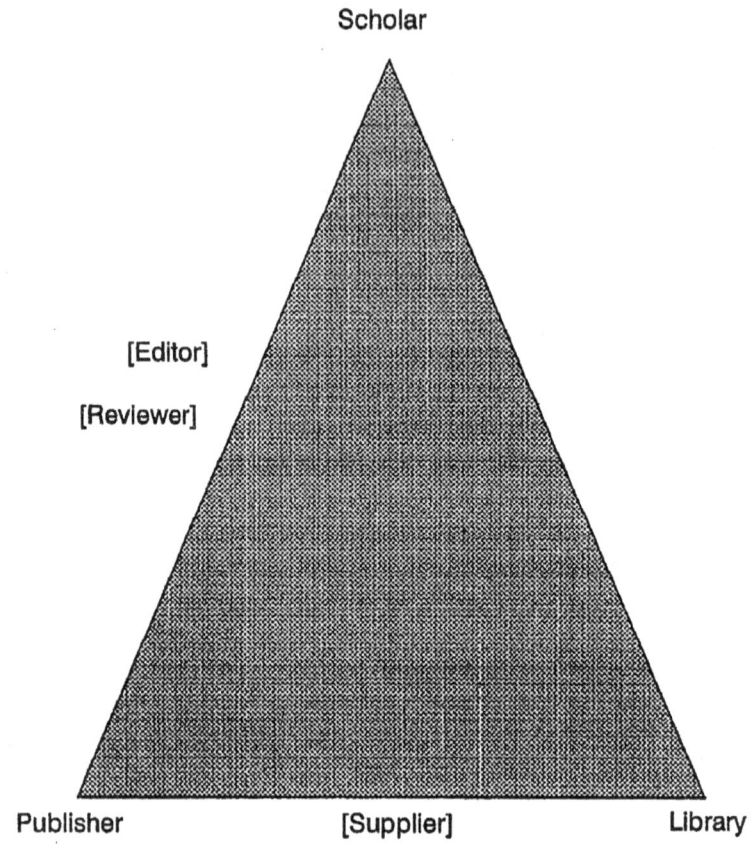

Figure 1

nals, and especially within that group, scientific and technological periodicals. A seminar previously organised by AACOBS in Brisbane in 1987 was largely motivated by the crisis which hit many libraries throughout this country in 1986 after the Australian dollar had been floated.

Because so much of our concern then was focussed on the value of the Australian dollar itself I was mildly surprised to discover first-hand, and within two months of having participated in the AACOBS Seminar on Acquisitions Rationalisation in Brisbane, that my colleagues in American libraries were *just* as preoccupied as we were with inflation in the price of printed information, particularly journals, . . . not in their case, however, motivated by a perception about the effect of the floating of their dollar. Indeed, if there was one theme evident as I went from place to place hearing about the problems of outrageous pricing policies it was the very definite view that in some way American libraries were being exploited by European publishers. This was seen as part of some larger economic conflict between the North American and European Community economic zones. It's worth a diversionary note here to record that in some of my reading of the literature of electronic publishing including the development in the United States of the National Research and Education Network and the Coalition for Networked Information, at least one of the motivations is economic nationalism. William Gray Potter, Director of Libraries at the University of Georgia stated in 1990:

> Some believe that there is a basic problem with a system that uses Federal dollars to subsidise research at American universities that is reported in journals published in Europe and then sold back to libraries at American universities whose budgets are also subsidised with Federal dollars.[1]

What sort of dollars are we looking at here? The Bowker Library and Booktrade Almanac for 1991 gives a figure of $530,542,000 expended in financial year 1989-90 by over 3,000 American academic libraries on periodicals. Figure 2 illustrates. Periodicals accounted for the largest single reported item of acquisitions expenditure, followed by books at $395 million. It is worth noting that in the same year expenditure on machine readable materials was just under $6 million, and on database fees a figure of $17.7 million, although it is unclear to me whether those database fees would include those paid to bibliographic utilities. Taken together the machine readable materials expenditure and the database fees represent something over 4% of dollars expended on periodicals.[2]

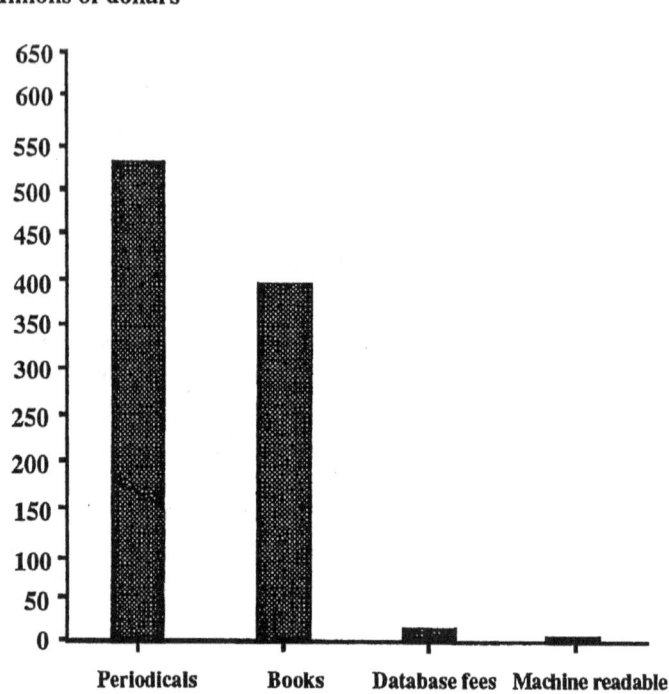

Figure 2 Acquisitions Expenditure - US Libraries 1989–90

The same source indicates that from 1983-89 books and periodicals for American academic libraries inflated by over 53%. Over the same period labour inflated by 30% and the average cost of non-book material went *down* by .2 of 1%. Of this latter and interesting figure video cassettes accounted for a 30% drop.

Library managers know that the containment of these costs and the general efficiency of systems for acquiring information are among their biggest if not *the* biggest challenges of the present. When the simple question has been asked–why year after year do the costs of printed information consistently, and apparently inexplicably, outstrip the CPI indexes for the nation in which the publishing has occurred?–the answers have not always been satisfactory. Perhaps that is because they have been piecemeal. I have heard library suppliers explain the concept of "twigging" in which increasingly specialised areas of knowledge become the basis for new titles, and periodicals that were once broad enough to contain or represent several branches of specialist knowledge are for some reason no longer adequate to the task. Perhaps there are others here who share my feeling of not being completely satisfied with such explanations.

One of the best expositions of the problem which I have come across in recent times is a discussion in the bulletin of the Medical Library Association, again in the States. In a discussion of journal pricing issues Arthur Hafner and colleagues make some telling points about competition.[3] Their main proposition is that as prices surge new titles appear, attracted by the prospect of taking profit in a market that appears to support rising prices. At some time later libraries and scholars react. When put under the hammer at their respective institutional levels there is always an inclination shared by both parties (i.e., the librarian and the academic) to hang on to tried and tested journals and not discard these in favour of new titles. So some new titles never really get going. What this means is that as prices rise, old and established titles are actually protected from competition. This is quite a different phenomenon to that which occurs in free markets for other commodities. It has to do with the uniqueness of any given title. In a sense each publisher of an established title has a form of monopoly simply because the information in each individual title cannot be regarded as being precisely duplicated anywhere else.

Other factors which have the effect of depressing competition include the process of twigging which I described earlier, and also the practice of dual subscription prices. Despite controversy among the libraries responsible for paying invoices dual pricing has generally speaking been (and despite misgivings) protected and respected by libraries. How many times have the people in this audience familiar with this aspect of librarianship declined to take donated titles because of the administrative overheads associated with them, compared to the simplicity of the institutional subscription–guaranteed to arrive on time despite the fact that it is four times the price?

And suppose the academic library concerned does take a radical view and decide to assist competition in the industry by cancelling established titles and promoting those taken on as new subscriptions in the last year or two. How much support would they get from their academic colleagues in such a project? The final point in insuring that extraordinary price rises actually diminish competition is that faculty members themselves (if given a choice) will seek always to publish in these same established titles which we know would be absolutely last on their own list of suggested cancellations . . . of course with the system of reward that operates in most Universities around the world there can be no question that I would prefer my paper on superconductivity to appear in *Nature* or the *Scientific American* rather than some completely new title that has just developed in the last two years.

If we accept then that these sometimes unmanageable economic pressures are brought about by the factors I have described so far there are two obvious issues which arise. The first of these concerns the role and behaviour of the original producers in the triangle, i.e., the authors and scholars, and the second concerns changes in forms of communication which might impinge on the worlds of all three.

THE SCHOLAR

Librarians in academic settings rarely tire of pointing out to various interested parties that they are the meat in the sandwich. Their academic communities do not understand why libraries are so expensive to run, and yet the very foundation on which academic careers are based is that of publishing in accepted forums to establish peer recognition and the validity of their scholarship. It is on this that academic careers and progression are based and on this that the welfare or the profitability of the third apex of our triangle, the publishers, is also based.

Is this problem generally recognised, i.e., by people other than librarians and some publishers who are feeling the pinch? Can something be done about it?

I think the answer to the first question is definitely yes . . . those who are responsible for running the higher education system *are* aware of this particular cost pressure, this recurrent problem of inflation. The answer to the second is complicated but I think that it is worth taking a deeper look at why people publish in the first place before we go on to look at the prognosis.

Most of us are familiar with the "publish or perish" syndrome. During the most dramatic years of the information explosion after the Second World War, and especially in the burgeoning social sciences, there was extraordinary publishing activity in scholarly journals and I am sure there are many here who have on more than one occasion queried the direction and the quality of that activity. Our own discipline of librarianship is a case in point. There can be spectacular differences between articles in different journals in our own field in terms of quality, original research, original contribution to knowledge and so on. But if we ask the basic question, "what is the primary motivation in publishing?" we come to some very fundamental human issues. I would like to illustrate this by way of example because the example concerned also relates to the way that people communicate within a particular discipline.

Just before Christmas in 1938 the German scientists Lise Meitner and Otto Frisch were walking in the country in Sweden just north of the city of Gothenburg. They were discussing some recent and inexplicable findings which had emerged from some work that they had been doing in Germany on the bombardment of atoms of uranium with neutrons. The moment of understanding of the significance of their work came between the two, the aunt and her nephew, sitting on a log with a pencil and an envelope. Then it was that they realised that the nucleus, under bombardment, was being split into two entities of almost equal mass, rather than being fragmented or "chipped" as previously thought. An associated finding was that the reason that elements higher than uranium on the Periodic Table had eluded detection was that the atomic nucleus had reached the point of inherent instability. Cautious at the extraordinary consequences of their discovery, it was discussed further after Christmas using the long distance telephone between Stockholm and Copenhagen heavily. Still cautious, they passed their results in front of the famous Danish physicist Niels Bohr who was about to leave for the United States. But it was not until the findings were published as a note in the letters to the editor of *Nature* in February 1939 that Frisch and Meitner could consider that their work was formalised and valid. It is doubtful that either of them were thinking of their careers in a "publish or perish" sense. Their determination was simply to see that their findings were validated, i.e., could be both perceived and accepted by peers around the world and that they then had the satisfaction of being recognised for their contribution to the store of knowledge in this area.[4]

What was extraordinary about this particular event of course, was that it was here that for the first time the word "fission" was used, there being a direct line of development from their understanding on the log in Sweden to the post-war nuclear age and all it has meant. What was even more extraordinary is that both scientists were German, the discovery was made within nine months of the outbreak of the Second World War, the journal of promulgation was the English journal *Nature*, with the scientists publishing in perfect English and its most concentrated discussion and readership occurred in North America.

Meitner and Frisch were not publishing because they were involved in some escalation of their academic careers. Indeed Meitner had, because she was Jewish, fled to Sweden only weeks before. What is more, she was by this time sixty years old.

The reason I digress with this story, apart from the fact that it is interesting in its own right, is that whatever systems are developed for scholarly communication in the future they must provide this quintessential requirement to validate and communicate in a way which is understood by all those who are part of the same enterprise. *Any system which fails to do this will not work.*

ELECTRONIC COMMUNICATION AS IT IS NOW

In an analysis of the way that physicists communicate in more recent days, Robert Allen outlined the various forms of communication which from his perspective as a subject specialist librarian he had observed.[5] These include oral forms of communication (from talks on a log to meeting at conferences), written communication whether in the form of a letter or an article in a refereed journal, and electronic communication including electronic mail, computer conferencing, electronic newsletters and electronic journals. One of the issues raised in Allen's analysis but not explicitly brought out by him is the degree to which current electronic forms of communication are acting as a substitute for the more *informal* modes of discourse between scholars. In other words while it is true that electronic mail, some things which we call electronic journals, electronic newsletters and computer conferences are becoming more frequently used, what kind of communication do they represent? I think it is clear at this stage that they represent Meitner and Frisch's talk on the log, long distance telephone calls and drafts of a paper. They do *not* represent that note to the journal, *Nature*.

Similarly much of the electronic publishing so called, that libraries are now investing in is simply the electronic replication of something in which the original means of production is no different to what it has been for many years. *Business Periodicals On Disk*, the largest single investment of my own institution, is a case in point.

There is no shortage of speculation about what the future might hold in electronic publishing, but I think that the distinction between "electronics in publishing" and electronic publishing is worth making and considering. Writing three years ago Anne Piternick (a Canadian academic) examined reasons why electronic journal publishing had by and large failed by the end of the 1980s to meet the predictions of those such as F.W. Lancaster. Says Piternick "the current publish or perish paradigm requires a printed, widely distributed format which is easily accessible to all."[6]

If we remove the word "printed" from Anne Piternick's sentence we have a statement which is now in its early stages of wide assessment and examination.

FUTURE DEVELOPMENTS AND THE ROLE OF THE STAKEHOLDERS

In the time since Piternick's rather cautious analysis, there has been no shortage of scenarios depicted in the literature on how scholarly communication should work in the 21st Century. There have been some rather interesting summit meetings reported between the various stakeholders in the system. The stakeholders include both commercial publishers and non commercial publishers. Indeed, a reported difficulty of some of them has been the difference in approach by librarians towards publishers who are in it for a profit and those who are not. In the years since 1989 there have been significant events affecting the library world primarily in North America in the first instance. One of these has been the discussion and somewhat tortuous development of the idea of the National Research and Education Network in the United States, and the other is the quite specific foundation of a new organisation called the Coalition for Networked Information which I referred to earlier. This coalition which draws representatives from three main groups has established a task force which now has over 140 members. The group has established working groups and two of these are specifically entitled "modernisation of scholarly publishing" and "transformation of scholarly communication."

The interesting thing about this development is that the contributing or sponsoring organisations which are the Association of Research Libraries, CAUSE (the Association for the Management of Information Technology in Higher Education) and EDUCOM are already heavily representative of, if not exclusively then substantially, libraries. And it is the influence of libraries on the future direction of publishing which has now reached a most interesting juncture. Said British publisher Neil Morley, when addressing a group of librarians, "as part of the library community, I doubt whether you realise your own power in shaping the future of my industry." It was Morley also who distinguished between electronics in publishing and electronic publishing, indicating that in theory at least the application of some forms of improved technology have made the enterprise of publishing itself more efficient and therefore potentially more profitable.[7]

So libraries, on whom a good number of scholarly publishers are dependent for their livelihood, have a significant role to play, particularly if they are highly organised through peak bodies. So too, authors. . . . There is the prediction made by some that the not always popular surrendering of ownership of intellectual property to publishers on the part of authors is challenged by new scenarios for scholarly communication. M. Stuart Lynn, Vice-President for Information Technologies at Cornell University recently suggested that new models of communication would put ownership of information back with the authors.[8]

It might be thought, if we refer to our original triangle that the apex of it which would be most seriously challenged in the event of an agreed shift from the printed periodical as the understood container for the process of scholarly validation and acceptance to some electronic ether is the publishers. Indeed, publishers have not been comfortable with the direction of discussion at some of the forums and colloquia which are written up in journals such as the *Serials Librarian*, *Library Acquisitions, Practice and Theory*, and so on. But consider our figures at the beginning of this discussion. It is clear that by far the largest investment, even in the early 90s in libraries, is in printed information. The shape of the library, the way it is organised, the sort of things that are done in it, is still part of a model which developed decades ago. If scholarly communication is going to radically shift its container base, *libraries will be as profoundly affected as publishers*. In a sense it is the authors, the scholars themselves, who have the most to gain by a major paradigm shift in the containers for the literature (for want of a better phrase). But to say this assumes rather a lot:

- it assumes that publishers are not themselves thinking deeply about the future actions which they might take to steer in directions which would preserve publishers' interests, and remember some publishing is very narrowly controlled by very wealthy people;
- it assumes that authors and scholars will act in some kind of concerted way;

- it assumes that the myriad of problems associated with copyright and intellectual ownership issues will be sorted out.

This is no proper mention of copyright in passing. I believe that many of the experiments which the advent of electronic publishing and high speed national and international networks will make possible, such the Royal Melbourne Institute of Technology's telelibrary, will realise their potential only when coordinated and concerted and understood action occurs on the issue of ownership and copyright.

CONCLUSION

I think that it is time in Australia that we got more organised on these issues. But it is hard for us to strike out on our own and in terms of our dependence on imported information it would be absurd to do so. Let's put this last point in perspective. It is worth noting that in the year 1986 (the latest for which UNESCO comparative figures are available) published output in the United States was something over 52,000 titles, the United Kingdom 58,000, in Germany 63,000, in the former USSR 83,000, and in Australia a mere 7,000. Figure 3 illustrates.[9] Our job in some respects is harder, because we must necessarily monitor and respond to developments such as the formation of the Coalition for Networked Information and the advent of NREN. But it is important to do so. Perhaps the Australian Vice-Chancellors Committee's working party on information resources would be a place to start. I believe the ultimate resolution of these issues will not develop, however, from laissez faire approaches.

It is sensible, finally, to agree with the President of Faxon (Richard Rowe) that "the future of scholarly publishing is not an issue of technology; it is an issue of economics and social policy."[10] And while the shape of our triangle is difficult to predict, i.e., we cannot tell in what way it will distort, distend or dissolve, one thing to me seems certain, it will take *more* than those players presently at its apexes to decide its ultimate shape. We should get moving–there is a lot to be done.

Figure 3   Published Output - Selected Country 1986

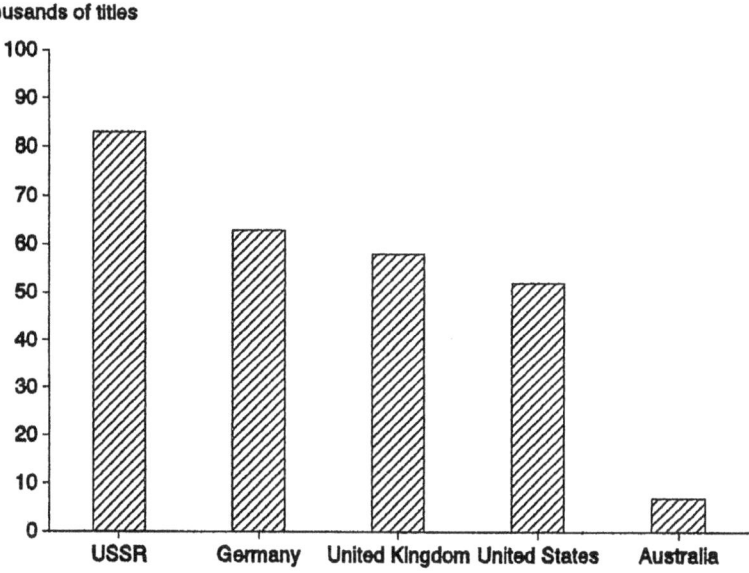

NOTES

1. Potter, William G., "The Growing Demand for Electronic Publishing," *Library Acquisitions, Practice and Theory*, 15(3), 1991; p 374.
2. *The Bowker Annual Library and Book Trade Almanac*, 36th edition, 1991; pp 382, 383.
3. Hafner, A.W., Podsadecki, T.J., and Whitely, W.P., "Journal Pricing Issues: An Economic Perspective," *Bulletin of the Medical Library Association*, 78(3), July 1990; pp 217-223.
4. Rhodes, Richard, *The Making of the Atomic Bomb* (NY: Simon and Schuster, 1986), pp 256-264.
5. Allen, Robert S., "Physics Information and Scientific Communication: Information Sources and Communication Patterns," *Science and Technology Libraries*, 11(3); pp 27-8.
6. Piternick, Anne, "Serials and New Technology, the State of the 'Electronic Journal,'" *Canadian Library Journal*, 46(2), April 1989; pp 93-94.
7. Morley, Neil, "The Future Pattern of Publishing," *Catalogue and Index*, 90/91 Autumn/Winter 1988; pp 14-16.

8. Michalak, Thomas J., and Kirk, Thomas, "Coalition for Networked Information Maps Directions," *College and Research Libraries News*, 52(4), April 1991; p 230.

9. *The Bowker Annual*, 1991; pp 444, 445.

10. Rowe, Richard, "The Economics of Scholarly Communication," *Library Acquisitions, Practice and Theory*, 13(4), 1989; p 427.

When the Electronic Journal Comes to the Campus

Carol Newton-Smith

For years as reference librarians we have done online searches and handed over lists of citations only to see researchers' faces fall when they realise that they still have to find the articles themselves. Now, with the arrival of the electronic journal at last we may be able to present the researcher with the full meal not just the menu. With the advent of AARNet (Australian Academic Research Network) we have easy access to the growing number of electronic journals available over the Internet. The electronic journal has arrived at the campus. What exactly are they? How do we find out about them? What are we going to do about them as reference librarians? Should we store them, and if so how? What are the implications for other sections of the library? These are some of the questions which have prompted this paper.

1. WHAT IS AN ELECTRONIC JOURNAL?

In this paper, the electronic journal is considered in a broad sense as any serial produced, published and distributed via an electronic medium. But, in the main, the paper will deal with those electronic journals freely available over the Internet.

2. ELECTRONIC VERSUS PAPER JOURNAL

There has been a lot of discussion recently on the news group PACS-L about the respective merits of each medium (PACS-

L@UHUPVM1.bitnet April/May under the subject heading "electronic versus paper"). The outcome would seem to be that both will probably coexist. Electronic journals have both advantages and disadvantages in comparison with the printed form.

2.1 Advantages

Instant access

Articles published in print journals can take months to reach the reader (Okerson 1991). Where ideas and technology are changing rapidly, this is not fast enough. The research done for this article was achieved through electronic means. Reading the *Public-Access Computer Systems Review* electronic journal, which arrives in the form of contents pages in my mail box, is wonderful because you know that if a title appeals you can get an instant copy of the full article with just an electronic mail message to the listserv. None of the frustrations of finding out which library has the journal and setting off on a tiresome hunt!

Issues can be unbundled

You only need to obtain those articles you want. In time hopefully you will only pay for what you need, which has interesting implications for authors who "repackage" old articles. It may be the scholar not the editor who makes the choice whether to obtain an article or not.

Issues are directly loadable into an electronic database

This makes them searchable, with advantages such as Boolean logic, and also transferable to other forms, for example to produce bibliographies.

Proofreading can be done by authors

Articles can be transferred in minutes via electronic mail for the author to proofread.

Economical of storage space

Electronic storage is much more efficient in terms of space than volumes on a shelf.

Environmentally friendly–less paper

It is recognised that recipients of an electronic journal may want a printout, but generally they will print only the articles they are interested in, not whole issues.

2.2 Disadvantages

Hardware and software are required

There is a great variety and no standardization.

Computer literacy is desirable

In fact computer phobia needs to be overcome for some individuals.

Peer review is less common

There are some electronic journals which are peer reviewed (Strangelove 1992) but most peer reviewed journals are still in print form.

Graphics are difficult to provide

ASCII format is no problem and most electronic journals available at this stage are in ASCII. Electronic transmission of graphics is a problem. The *Journal of Technology Education* sends a Postscript file for graphics, but Gail McMillan (1991) remarks that "when Postscript has been used for electronic journals, file transfer problems between computers have resulted."

Copyright is uncertain

Everyone is unsure about the copyright situation and the publishers need to be able to protect their investments and the author's rights to an income.

Archives are hard to maintain

Electronic media are easily open to alteration and loss, and the security of archives is a problem which needs to be resolved.

Authors are at present more reluctant to publish only in electronic form

3. TYPES OF ELECTRONIC JOURNAL

Electronic publishing has been classified in various ways (Wang 1987). It is useful to examine some of these classifications to establish some of the characteristics of electronic journals.

3.1 Location (Working Group on Electronic Publishing 1983, Hills 1985)

Where is the publication physically situated? It may be centralized, decentralized or a hybrid. Centralized publication is when online full text journals are stored on a remote computer with access via dialup or leased line. *Current Clinical Trials* was recently established in this manner with no facility for items to be sent electronically. This caused some discussion in PACS-L (Bauer 1991). Decentralized publication is when stored information is sold in packages. CD-ROMs and electronic journals distributed via the Internet are examples of decentralized publication. Hybrid electronic publishing is the halfway house. The Pergamon InfoLine Video Patsearch system is an example. Videodisc technology is linked by microcomputer to the mainframe information retrieval system. A search is made of the bibliographic database and the text and drawings of the listed patent can be called up from a local videodisc.

3.2 Products (Cuadra 1981)

The type of product is another way of looking at electronic publishing. Products may be regarded as primary or secondary. Primary journals are those that contain source or full text material, such as the *MeckJournal*. A secondary journal contains only the references or citations. *Current Cites* is an example of this. It can be frustrating in Australia to receive electronically citations to articles which themselves appear only in print. There is usually a considerable time lag until the receipt of the printed article. However there is always electronic mail. I saw a reference in a recent issue of *Current Cites* (Vol 3., no. 4, April 1992) to an article by Charles Bailey entitled "Network-based electronic serials" (Bailey 1992b). The article was in a printed issue not yet received in Australia, but an electronic message to the author resulted in a copy arriving very quickly.

3.3 Availability of Print Products (Working Group on Electronic Publishing 1983)

Is a printed product available or not? Journals may be classified as parallel or fully electronic journals. The *Electronic Journal of the Astronomical Society of the Atlantic* has an interesting policy. It states that "articles which appear in the *EJSA* may also be published in the *Journal of the ASA*" so the journal fits exactly into neither category but is a kind of hybrid.

3.4 Types of Technologies Applied (Raitt 1987)

Libraries mostly classify journals by the types of technology applied and treat them differently, according to the technology used. Electronic journals come in a variety of technologies: online, CD-ROM (e.g., *Business Periodicals OnDisc*), or disk (e.g., *Current Contents*). At Curtin University all journals received in the library in whatever form are recorded in the serials catalogue, but how they are handled depends on their form. CD-ROM journals like *Business Periodicals OnDisc* are stored in the electronic information area, separate from print serials or microfiche serials. Online journals available in full text are usually available via the reference staff but these are not considered to be "received." The reference staff attempt to keep Inter-Library Loans staff up to date with all new sources of online journals.

3.5 Price

There are several ways that an electronic journal may be acquired: subscription, license, payment for single articles, or free distribution. Ann Okerson (1991) suggests that by the year 2000 the subscription model will wane, and the use of license and single article models will grow.

3.6 Peer Review

There has been a lot of discussion on the "Net" about the value of peer review and the effect of its absence (Harnad 1992). Of the thirty or more current electronic journals, only about ten (Strangelove 1992) are refereed or lightly refereed.

Electronic journals provide examples of all the different characteristics of electronic publishing. In the remainder of this paper, however, the ones that will be discussed are those available free via the Internet in a decentralised form.

4. HOW TO FIND OUT ABOUT ELECTRONIC JOURNALS

4.1 Directories

Michael Strangelove produced the first "Directory of electronic journals and newsletters" in 1991 and a second edition 1992. It is produced both in print and electronic form. The print form is avail-

able from the Association of Research Libraries ($10.00 for members, $20.00 non-members + $5.00 for foreign–non American–postage). Electronically the directory is available in ASCII form from the following location:
listserv@uottawa
Leave the subject line blank and put the following message in the main body of the text:

   get ejourn11 directry
   get ejournl2 directry

4.2 Electronic Meetings

There are general library meetings like PACS-L (Public-Access Computer Systems Forum) which covers all computer systems that libraries make available to their patrons. Membership of PACS-L includes issues of electronic serials like *Current Cites* and *PACS-L Review*, and PACS-L advises of new electronic journals that are issued. PACS-L also sends out the best source for electronic meetings which is the publication (electronic!) put out by Charles Bailey entitled "Library-Oriented Computer Conferences and E-Serials."

There are other electronic meetings which are serials specific. One of these is SERIALST (Serials in Libraries Discussion Forum) which was established in October 1990 to serve as an informal forum for most aspects of serials processing in libraries. It is a moderated list (meaning that someone scans the messages first which removes a lot of rubbish). Recent topics have included: formal versus informal serials instruction, subscription procedures, serials budgets and so on.

Another serials specific meeting specialises in electronic serials, VPIEJ-L (Scholarly Electronic Journals Electronic Publishing Issues). Topics for discussion on VPIEJ-L include formats, access to e-journals, and creation of e–journals. One of the goals of the list is to provide better feedback from users to creators.

A useful source of new electronic meetings is the group NEW-LISTS@ndsuvm1. It is also available on NEWS as news.announce.newgroups.

4.3 Journals

Citations for Serial Literature is an electronic journal whose purpose is to identify literature related to the serials industry. It publishes the table of contents and abstracts when available for articles related to the serials industry. Currently this database includes the table of contents for some issues of:

> *Newsletter on Serials Pricing Issues*
> *Serials Review*
> *Library Acquisitions, Practice and Theory.*
> To subscribe send an email message to:
> listserv@mitvma.mit.edu
> leave the subject line blank and in the body of the message put:
> sub sercites <your name>

There are also print journals that discuss electronic publishing, such as *Electronic Publishing Review. Serials Review* now includes a column entitled "Electronic Journal Forum" (Langschied 1992).

4.4 Indexing Services

Indexing services are beginning to include electronic journals. ERIC has tackled the indexing of *New Horizons in Adult Education* (Langschied, 1992). The *MLA Bibliography* also includes electronic journals (Uchitelle, 1992).

4.5 Standard Serials Directories

Ulrich's International Periodicals Directory 1991/92 includes lists of "Serials available on CD-ROM" and "Serials available Online" but as yet no electronic journals available via the Internet are listed.

5. WHAT TO DO WITH THEM WHEN THEY ARRIVE

Electronic journals should be freely available to academics in a way that will permit them to:

- access journals easily
- be notified when a new issue arrives
- search by keyword
- use Boolean logic to refine searches
- have easy access to archives
- have them available at their desk
- use any platform-dumb terminal, Mac, IBM
- easily copy them into their own personal system where interest warrants it.

This last item usually depends on the type of equipment used for access. A PC or a Mac makes the transfer possible while a dumb terminal means access only to the mainframe facilities. To cater for the lowest common denominator, i.e., a dumb terminal, the mainframe facilities should be as complete as possible.

Existing scenario

The existing scenario at Curtin University is that academics subscribe to journals on an individual basis. The issues come into their mailboxes and academics are notified of each issue as it arrives. Any platform can be used for access. But there are no facilities for searching in mail and, while issues can be accumulated as an archive, its organization is not easy. The existing scenario also causes storage problems, since an individual's block allocation on the central Vax machine is limited, while the networks may also clog up as several academics obtain the same files from distant computers using ftp (file transfer protocol).

A joint research proposal between the Library, Computing Centre and the School of Information Systems to investigate these issues is being undertaken. The project title is "Evaluation of full text electronic journal server technologies for use at Curtin University." Several different storage and access options have been identified and are being given preliminary tests, and others are also being investigated. It is intended to use staff members who already subscribe to electronic journals as a test group. The group of staff will be divided up into smaller test groups to evaluate the different technologies.

The proposed options at this stage are as follows.

5.1 Provide a front-end (e.g., IRAS–Information Resources Access System) and use telnet to a remote storage, e.g., MeckJournal.

IRAS is being developed by Deirdre Stanton of Murdoch University and Kaye Stott of the University of Western Australia, using Hypertext software from Peter Scott and Earl Fogel of the University of Saskatchewan, Canada. The aim of IRAS is to provide an easy front-end to enable academics to use the resources of AARNet/Internet on any platform from a menu interface which would hide the details. For example the academic could choose "*MeckJournal*" from a list of electronic journals available, and the computer would engage in the following steps to connect him without him being aware:

>   telnet to nisc.jvnc.net
>   type nicol [lower case] at the logon prompt no password is needed
>   select MC92 from the preliminary nicol menu

Access would be simple but dependent on gateways to overseas networks which can be slow at peak times. There would be no notification of new issues in this system. Searching is possible by keyword but no Boolean facilities are available. Archival access is available but dependent on the remote storage policy. Any platform can be used for access and it is available from the desktop. Only a few journals are available in this fashion at present. Those that are available are all on different platforms so there is no ease of use. A Gopher interface (Alberti 1992) is also being considered.

5.2 Usenet NEWS Database on University Mainframe

Curtin University has a Usenet NEWS database so some journals are already available from the feed (e.g., *Psycoloquy* in news group sci.psychology.digest) and others could be set up. As Gail McMillan points out, "the Usenet interface is not ideal, but it's a good first approximation, and it already exists" (McMillan 1992). It is relatively easy to establish a local news database and feed in any electronic journals not obtainable from elsewhere. Access would be easy but there would be no notification of a new issue. Searching on a NEWS database is limited to string search and can be tedious. Archiving could be a problem as most universities only retain items for a limited period on a NEWS database.

5.3 WAIS Database on University Mainframe

WAIS (Wide Area Information Server) is primarily the work of Thinking Machines Corporation, a leading U.S. supercomputer manufacturer (Hooper 1991). Curtin University has a WAIS server operating on a Sun Unix system in the Computing Centre with two experimental databases on it: SCOR (Software and Courseware Online Reviews), a database of software reviews compiled by the Computing Centre over the years, and Chemical Engineering Current Contents, provided by one of the lecturers, Dr. Martyn Ray.

The exciting thing about WAIS is that it is a protocol which allows users to search and access different types of information from a single interface. The information can be anything from text to graphics and can reside anywhere on all sorts of systems. It is an extension of the ANSI Z39.50 information retrieval protocol.

User workstations can access the WAIS server using WAIS client software on their local Mac, X Windows, or PC, or using SWAIS at Thinking Machines (telnet quake.think.com). The Mac client software is far superior to using SWAIS, however. Once you have a WAIS client you specify the source(s) to search on. Then you ask the source a query. At present, this means keywords. The documents come back ranked according to the weights, percentages of each word in the document. You can ask for "other documents like this one." You can also set up SDI type queries and your "client" will go out and search the specified source databases at specified intervals for any new documents.

Local WAIS databases would probably be set up for those journals to which we wished to subscribe, but the software allows databases anywhere in the world to be searched by the same interface. It is possible that the databases could be automatically updated using the SDI type facility of WAIS. Access and search are easy with client software on a Mac or PC. In the research proposal, programming is planned for issue notification to an academic's mailbox. Searching is by keyword(s) but retrieval is ranked. One of the big pluses of the WAIS solution is that, if Curtin sets these databases up, they will be available throughout Australia and worldwide.

5.4 PC-Based Local Area Network

Storage and public access could be provided by expanding the PC-based local area network in the Library. Since early 1991 we have had a number of workstations (currently 12) on a network which provides access to 21 CD-ROMs (12 titles). As well as the CD-ROMs there is also the full text of the transcripts of the Western Australian Royal Commission on Government Business Activities, available as a database using ISYS full text retrieval software. Images attached to documents can also be viewed with ISYS, which will be useful for electronic journals containing graphics. An ISYS database will hold up to about 2000 million words (about 10 times the size of a CD-ROM).

Once connection is made from the LAN to the campus-wide network, access for academics on campus should be easy, through a choice on a menu, though outside access would be very unlikely, because of the CD-ROMs on the network. Issues would be loaded into the database in the library so that academics could be notified by electronic mail when a new issue arrives. The main advantage of the ISYS solution is the sophistication of the searching which includes Boolean logic and proximity operators. Archives would be under the library's control. The main disadvantage is that the library's electronic information network is not yet connected to the campus-wide network and access is currently only available in the library.

5.5 Other Possibilities

One of the academic staff in the School of Information Systems at Curtin University, Heinz Dreher, is developing a Hypertext solution which has strong possibilities. Another solution which has been used elsewhere is Vax NOTES (Drew 1992). But the Curtin University Computing Centre commented that NOTES is not as good as NEWS, only runs on a Vax, and must be paid for on use. Nor would it be possible to get NOTES from outside in the same way as NEWS (Hooper 1992).

6. CONCLUSION

Why should electronic journals succeed where so many other alternatives to the scientific journal have failed? Anne Piternick (1989) has reviewed early attempts to find alternatives to the scientific journal. These experiments failed because they were externally imposed, scholars were not interested in writing for electronic media and they were unwilling to read it. There are many problems to be overcome (Bailey 1992b) but electronic journals are now freely available via AARNet and academics are not only reading them but creating them. Are we as librarians going to manage the electronic information that scholars are going to want? Will the future be a feast or a chaotic technical smorgasbord?

BIBLIOGRAPHY

Alberti, B. [et al.] (1992) "The Internet Gopher protocol: a distributed document search and retrieval protocol" Available via ftp to host boombox.micro.umn.edu (directory pub/gopher/gopher_protocol; file name protocol.txt).

Bailey, C.W. (1992a) "Electronic serials and related topics: a brief bibliography" (lib3@uhupvm1.bitnet). Message on VPIEJ-L@VTM1.BITNET 24/4/92.

Bailey, C.W. (1992b) "Network-based electronic serials" *Information Technology and Libraries* Vol. 11 no. 2 p.29-35.

Bauer, M. (1991) "Archival/retrieval of electronic journals" (malcolm@clarity.princeton.edu). Message on PACS-L@UHUPVM1.bitnet 18/10/91.

Cuadra, C.A. (1981) "A brief introduction to electronic publishing" *Electronic Publishing Review* Vol. 1 no. 1 p.29-34.

Drew, W.E. (1992) "Re: Patron access to electronic journals" (drewwe@snymorva.cs.snymor.edu). Message on PACS-L@uhupvm1.bitnet 5/3/92.

Harnad, S. (1992) "Peer review and the Net" (harnad@princeton.edu). Message on PACS-L@UHUPVM1.bitnet 14/4/92.

Hills, S. (1985) "Electronically published material and the archival library" *Electronic Publishing Review* Vol. 5 no. 1 p.63-69.

Hooper, T. (1992) "Storage/access of electronic journals" (chooper@dialix.oz.au). Personal electronic mail message 30/3/92.

Kellam, J. (1991) "WAIS, a sketch of an overview" (composer@Beyond.Dreams.ORG). Available for anonymous ftp from hosthydra.uwa.ca (directory libsoft; filename wais.txt).

Langschied, L. (1992) "Indexing electronic journals" (langschied@zodiac.bitnet). Message on PACS-L@UHUPVM1.bitnet 8/4/92.

McMillan, G. (1991) "Embracing the electronic library: one library's plan" *Serials Librarian* Vol. 21 nos. 2/3 p.97-108.

Okerson, A. (1991) "The electronic journal: what, whence and when?" *The Public Access Computer Systems Review* Vol. 2, no.1 p. 5-24.

Okerson, A. (1992) "Directory of e-journals, newsletters, lists PressRelease" (okerson@umdc.bitnet). Message on PACS-L@UHUPVM1.bitnet 1/4/92.

Piternick, A.B. (1989) "Attempts to find alternatives to the scientific journal: a brief review" *Journal of Academic Librarianship* Vol. 15 no. 5 p.260-266.

Piternick, A.B. (1991) "Electronic serials: realistic or unrealistic solution to the journal 'crisis'?" *Serials Librarian* Vol. 21 nos. 2/3 p. 15-31.

Raitt, D. (1987) "Electronic publishing: its status and acceptance" In: *Proceedings of the Institute of Information Scientists Annual Conference*, 24-27 June 1986, Peebles, Scotland.

Strangelove, M. (1992) "Peer reviewed networked e-serials" (441495@acadvm1.uottawa.ca). Message on PACS-L@UHUPVM1.bitnet 2/2/92.

Uchitelle, D. (1992) "Indexing of electronic journals" (mlaod@cuvmb.bitnet). Message on PACS-L@UHUPVM1.bitnet 8/4/92.

Wang, C. (1987) "Electronic publishing and its impact on print publishing and other selected library materials: a review, proposal, and design for further research" *The Electronic Library* Vol. 5 no. 2 p.86-92.

Working Group on Electronic Publishing (1983) "The impact of electronic publishing" *Electronic Publishing Review* Vol. 3 no. 4 p.291-302.

Access to Journal Information and the Impact of New Technologies

Anne H. Newell

Libraries within the higher education sector are experiencing

- continued growth in student numbers, particularly postgraduate students,
- an increasing number of research concentrations being introduced,
- the incorporation of information skills and research skills training into both undergraduate and postgraduate courses,
- as well as the combined effect of escalating serials inflation and the increasing number of new journal startups outstripping acquisitions budgets.

The services offered to assist users in locating bibliographic citations for journal articles have never been more heavily used by students at all levels. It is also apparent that they are preferring to use CD-ROM services to assist them rather than print indexes and abstracts. The "Pile-up at the reference desk"[1] attributed to the introduction of CD-ROM services is now a common phenomenon.

Further, our document supply services providing access to journal information not owned by the library or not located at the user's home campus are being overwhelmed. We know our interlibrary loan services are having difficulty meeting the growing demand for document supply resulting from the increasing numbers of postgraduate students. This is particularly true for the newer universities. Similar pressures are also being placed upon our special reciprocal loan arrangements with other libraries in the region and the library's internal inter-campus services.

As many university libraries are experiencing similar trends in both Australia and the United States, it is worthwhile investigating whether our observations are an accurate reflection of the needs for journal information by library patrons.

THE QUEENSLAND UNIVERSITY OF TECHNOLOGY ENVIRONMENT

CD-ROM Services Currently Offered

At QUT, access to CD-ROMs is available either by using stand alone workstations located near the reference desks on all campuses or the two campus-based CD-ROM networks. At the Gardens Point Campus, there is a separate facility referred to as the Public Access Database facility which is located near the Reference Desk. This facility has 7 stand alone PC's, with an additional workstation connected to the LAN maintained by the Computer Based Education Section. Currently, 80 workstations are available on the NOVELL local area network. Library patrons access 10 different CD-ROM titles on this network made possible through the use of OPTINET. Examples of titles networked include Medline, Social Sciences Index and six of the Wilsondisc databases.[2]

In total, QUT subscribes to 40 CD-ROM services that are available for patron use. Of these, approximately 30 are indexes and abstracts. CD-ROM services offering full-text journals include Business Periodicals OnDisk and Computer Select, with IEEE/IEE Publications OnDisk being considered for 1992. To date, no hard copy indexes and abstracts have been cancelled when the parallel CD-ROM service has been purchased.

At Kelvin Grove, a small CD-ROM network consisting of 3 workstations is also in operation. On all other campuses, stand alone workstations are available. Currently, there is no dial-in access to CD-ROM databases.

Future Access to CD-ROMs

The CD-ROM services were introduced prior to the amalgamation of the Queensland Institute of Technology and the Carseldine,

Kedron Park and Kelvin Campuses of the Brisbane College of Advanced Education in 1990. Post-amalgamation, there has naturally developed a pressing need for cross-campus access to CD-ROMs. In response to this demand, QUT is planning a library LAN with the file server connected to the ethernet backbone so that PC's distributed throughout the five[3] campuses may interrogate CD-ROM databases.

Serials Usage at QUT

It is evident from both backlogs in re-shelving of serials as well as patron feedback that our serials collections are being used extensively by undergraduate students, postgraduate students and staff. Further, our document supply services, by which I am referring to our intercampus loan, special reciprocal loan and interlibrary loan services, are unable to cope with the escalating demand. Growth in ILL borrowing for both Gardens Point and Kelvin Grove campuses from 1990 to 1991 rose by over 20% (i.e.,+ 20% for GP and +27% for KG).

The pressures on user education to teach students how to locate journal information earlier in their courses, and in particular requests for CD-ROM instruction, are mounting. The outcome being more sophisticated library users needing a range of resources to locate journal articles, and a consequent increase in journal usage. There has been an increased load on reference services generally, with CD-ROM inquiries taking up to 24% of the inquiries on the Reference Desk.

Electronic Journals

As with most university libraries, QUT is still coming to terms with the whole issue of electronic journals and the potential impact upon library services. At this stage, I simply want to mention that there is a working party established to formulate recommendations on the following.

    i. selection and retention of E-journals,
    ii. storage i.e., on the VAX or the Data General or the DEC,

iii. access and availability, in terms of

    (a) access to E-journals selected and therefore stored at QUT
    (b) as well as 'availability records' for titles on the networks (AARNet, INTERNET, JANET),

iv. and training needs for both academic and library staff.

SURVEY METHODOLOGY

Survey Objectives

I designed a survey instrument to meet the following objectives:

1. To identify preferred methods used to locate journal information.

Whether	print indexes and abstracts
	CD-ROM databases
	full-text CD-ROM services
	online databases
or	electronic journals available on the networks (i.e., AARNet, INTERNET, JANET)

2. To assess the perceived level of demand for current serials and back issues looking at both

    (a) a cross section of subject disciplines taught at QUT
    (b) as well as the different categories of library patrons, be they undergraduate students, postgraduate students, academic staff or general staff.

3. To evaluate the success of QUT collections and document supply services in meeting the journal information needs of the different client groups.

Survey Instrument

Approximately 700 survey forms were distributed across the four campuses of Carseldine, Gardens Point, Kedron Park and Kelvin

Grove. QUT's eight faculties were therefore targeted–the Faculties of Arts, Built Environment and Engineering, Business, Education, Health, Information Technology, Law and Science. The different user groups were identified as:

UNDERGRADUATE	POSTGRADUATE	STAFF
Year 1	Diploma	Academic
Years 2-3	Master	General
Years 4+	Doctorate	

The survey form was divided into three sections. **Section A** addressed preferred methods of locating journal information as well as whether users were successful in finding their journal articles. **Section B** covered an evaluation of CD-ROMs including users' likes and dislikes. Patrons were also asked to comment on any problems experienced in accessing CD-ROMs, both via single workstations and networked PC's. Further, questions regarding use of full-text CD-ROM databases and topical issues such as payment for services and the cancelling of hard copy journals were raised. **Section C** looked at the importance of journal information to the different categories of users and issues of access to journal information whether or not owned by the library. Patrons were asked to indicate their need for back issues as well as their level of usage of document supply services.

Distribution of the Survey

Over 50% of survey instruments distributed were returned. The ideal sample size for a representative sample of 384 returns was achieved, giving a probability of 95% that the error of estimation was less than 5%.

Survey forms were distributed firstly, to those who actually enter the library, with forms being made available at Information Desks on all campuses. Secondly, a systematic distribution was intended to capture academic staff with a random mail out. In addition, class groups were also targeted through liaison with academic staff in order to capture both library and non-library users.

ANALYSIS OF SURVEY RESPONSES AND KEY FINDINGS

The results of the survey were analysed by running SPSS. I will report here on the key findings under what I see to be some of the major issues within the context of the impact of new technologies.

Has Technology Added to the Pressures Placed Upon Libraries in Providing Access to Journal Information?

There is no doubt that "CD-ROM has significantly changed the way in which library users access information. Patrons have quickly and enthusiastically adopted the technology as an exciting alternative to print and online. They appreciate the convenience, ease of use and greater degree of control of the search process."[4]

At the same time, libraries are now offering an increasing number of computerised systems for searching and retrieving bibliographic citations to journal articles. Various models are now developing, with libraries often providing users with more than one option. Options such as

i. online database searching using, for example, BRS DIALOG AUSINET STN or ORBIT
ii. CD-ROM services, some of which are providing access to full-text journal articles
iii. mounting journal article citation databases, such as the Wilson tapes, on local library computer systems
iv. using the academic networks such as AARNET and the INTERNET to access remote databases and e-journals
v. or developing in-house databases, such as the IREL database, maintained by the QUT Kedron Park campus.

It is not surprising that the library patrons of the nineties are perceived as being 'more self-sufficient, sophisticated and demanding.' User education has played a significant role in raising the sophistication of library users who are now demanding more services to meet their needs.

This raises the question, WHAT DO PATRONS USE MOST

FREQUENTLY TO LOCATE JOURNAL INFORMATION AND HOW USEFUL DO THEY FIND THESE DIFFERENT MEANS?

Of the respondents, 36% indicated they would use CD-ROM 'always' or 'often.' Next most popular were print indexes and abstracts (24.6%), followed by online search services (21.1%), then full-text CD-ROM databases (20%), and lastly e-journals (4.7%)[5] (See Graph 1).

When looking at these results, it is important to note that online services at QUT are offered at a subsidised rate to academic staff and postgraduate students, as well as undergraduate students required to complete a final year project. A restricted number of databases are also offered to undergraduate students free of charge. Therefore, all categories of users are valid. Further, full-text CD-ROM services are only available in the disciplines of business and information technology. And so, in terms of the total sample, full-text CD-ROMs still rated highly in users' preferences.

To look at the graph again, while CD-ROM is used most often, more students are familiar with the print version than electronic alternatives. Only 31.1% of respondents had never used print indexes and abstracts. Whereas 39.6% were unfamiliar with CD-ROM databases, 47.9% with online search services and 54.3% with the CD-ROM full-text databases. With regard to e-journals, I checked responses against category of user, as access would only be available to academic staff and postgraduate students with a VAX account. Following from this, 79% of valid users had never used an e-journal. So, surprisingly, as no formal training courses have been conducted across campuses for AARNET, 21% of academic staff or postgraduate students were aware of the availability of e-journals and how to access them.

Respondents were also required to make a value judgement in assessing the 'usefulness' of the different methods available for locating journal information. Again, CD-ROM featured as being considered the most useful means of locating journal articles with 50.5% ranking this source as very useful or useful. Online search services were second in popularity (46.3%), followed by print indexes and abstracts (42.1), full-text CD-ROM databases (38.3%) and e-journals (10.3%). It is evident that the electronic alternatives were generally preferred to the print option (See Graph 2).

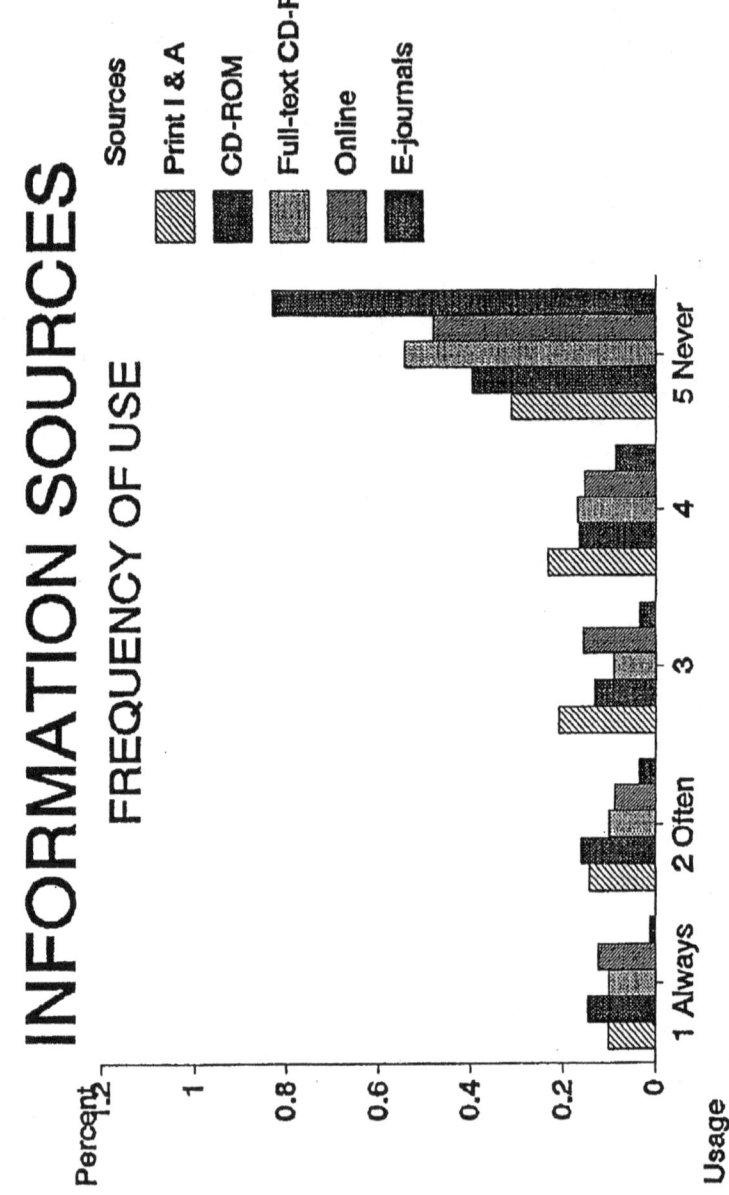

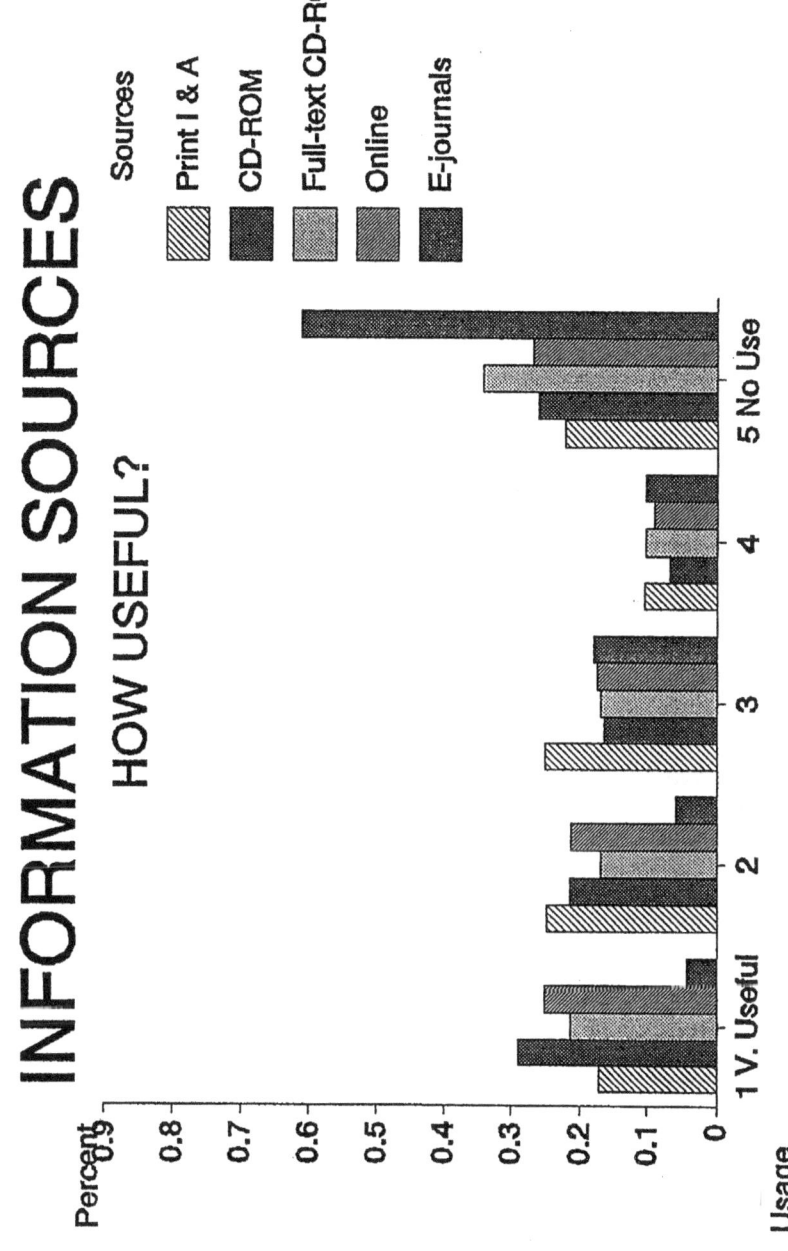

WHY ARE THE ELECTRONIC ALTERNATIVES PREFERRED? Respondents were asked what they liked best about using CD-ROM databases.

Quickly provides me with the information I need	35.2%
Easier to use than print indexes and abstracts	28.3%
Saves me looking elsewhere for information	22.3%
I like experimenting with new technology	9.1%

The results support other surveys conducted in the United States where the main benefit is seen to be the time factor. CD-ROM services are also more flexible. As one postgraduate student responded:

> [The CD-ROMs] have allowed me to define my topic more clearly, given me a quick knowledge of the journals in my research area, and given me a broad overview of topics related to my area.

What users disliked about CD-ROMs was foremost the problem of access to the databases they needed for their research or study. When respondents were requested to indicate their dislikes, the results were as follows:

The CD-ROM is not available when I need it	8.6%
The printing and/or downloading facilities are not sufficient for my needs	17.4%
I find it difficult to use them	10.6%
I am uncomfortable with new technology	2.7%
Other	50.8%

With the problem of access being anticipated, respondents were asked to identify which databases they had difficulty accessing. Most users expressed concerns with databases available on stand alone workstations, such as ERIC, AUSTROM and BPO.

ERIC	20.8%	MEDLINE	9.0%
AUSTROM	20.3%	COMPENDEX	6.1%
BPO	15.1%	CINAHL	5.7%
COMPUTER SELECT	9.0%		

The networked services rated amongst the lowest in terms of access.

IS NETWORKING ALL CD-ROMS THE ANSWER TO SOLVING ACCESS PROBLEMS?

I found that 54.6% of respondents had not used the CBE facility, which provides access to networked CD-ROMs, as they were simply not aware of this facility. At the same time, 17.6% of users preferred to use the workstations located near the reference desk where they were able to seek assistance. Of the 'other' reasons given for disliking CD-ROMs, one of the most common was in relation to response time, especially when the network is being heavily used. From our experiences at QUT, further corroborated by tests conducted by UMI, it would appear that response time for networked CD-ROMs tends to deteriorate when there are 10 to 12 simultaneous users.

Of course, these are issues of concern when planning expansion of networks, particularly when considering dial-in access. The physical location of CD-ROM facilities should also be carefully planned if we are to encourage maximum usage. The demand for remote access to CD-ROM facilities or networks is escalating. The following student response is indicative of this:

> I'd much rather [be able to search CD-ROMs] in the faculty/ school postgraduate room than in the crowded library.

At the same time, networking of all CD-ROMs is unattainable for most libraries due to the prohibitive cost structures applied by some producers. Networking of all CD-ROM titles is also not warranted. As with print indexes and abstracts, usage patterns vary. Apart from cost, licence agreements may also be an impediment to networking when there are needs for dial-in access and multi-campus access.

Another of the common complaints with regard to CD-ROM databases is the variety of software being released. For instance, in order to conduct a comprehensive search a user may need to be familiar with a number of different search engines such as silver platter, proquest, dialog or wilsonline.

And yet, it would appear unlikely that producers will agree to standardise search capabilities as the search engine is usually the distinctive feature of the product. Even though, such standardisation would be of great benefit to libraries and their users.

How Successful are Patrons in Locating Journal Articles Where Citations Had Been Retrieved Using Electronic Sources?

While we have identified that library patrons find electronic sources more useful in locating journal citations, the question of how successful they are in then locating the journal article needs to be addressed. The student or academic has, through using the sophisticated search capabilities of either CD-ROMs or online search services, been able to formulate a search strategy directly suited to their needs using key words and boolean logic, but are they able to locate the actual articles?

My original hypothesis was that users would successfully locate journal articles for which they have found citations up to 50% of the time. This was based upon experiences with users at the Information Desk. The response was slightly more promising than this, with the success rate being 56%. When users were unsuccessful it was primarily for the following reasons (See Graph 3).

i. Found the title in the catalogue, but QUT does not hold the issue I want — 53.4%
ii. Unable to locate the issue on the shelves — 39.3%
iii. Unable to find the journal title in the catalogue — 38.0%
iv. Do not know how to use the catalogue to find journals — 24.5%

These results indicate, that QUT has insufficient back runs of serials to meet the needs of a significant number of patrons. This of course will not be a surprise to many. However, it is interesting to note that the greater pressure is on depth in the collection and not

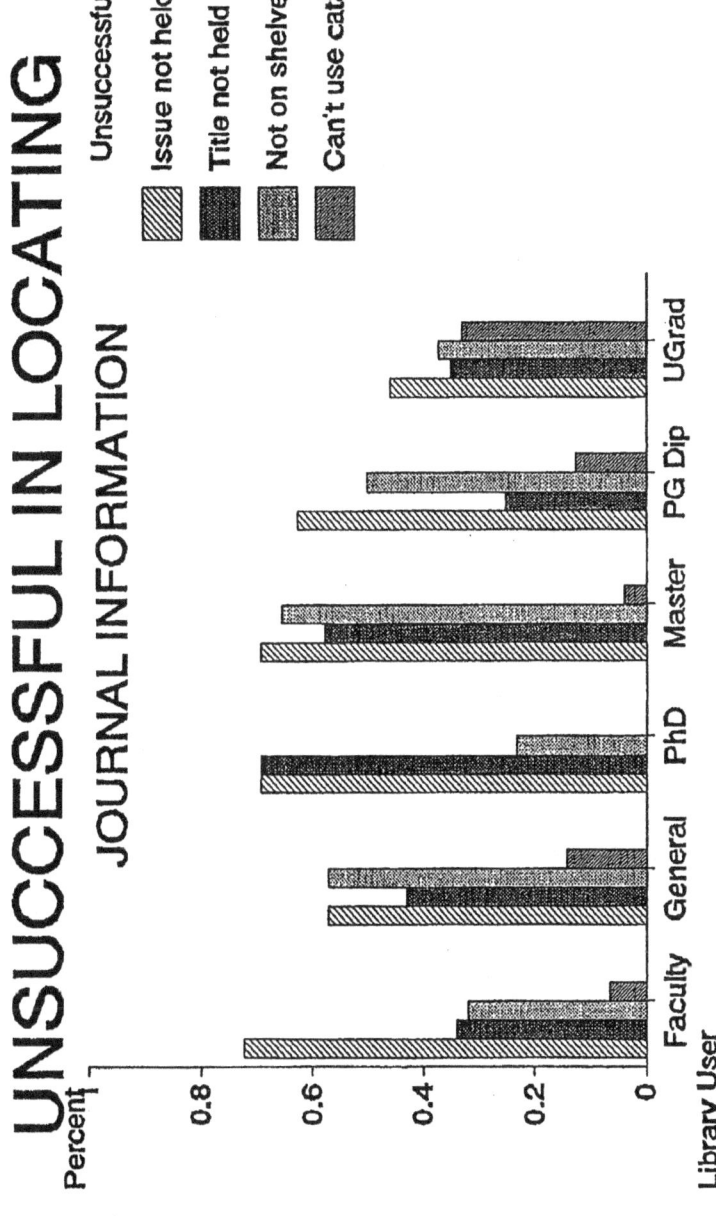

breadth of titles. It is also the first data we have obtained to illustrate how heavily the serials collection is being used. For close to 40% of the sample, the information they required was held at QUT but they were unable to locate the issue on the shelves. As serials at QUT are not for loan, then this result is only attributable to usage. Finally, I would expect that a quarter of the population being unable to use the catalogue to find journals to be higher than one would normally expect, due to the introduction of a new library system (URICA 2000) at the beginning of 1992.

In analysing faculty responses with regard to failure in finding the journal articles, the majority indicated the greatest problem was that QUT did not hold the particular issue they needed, not that QUT did not hold the title. Most faculties, including Business, Education, Health, Information Technology and Law, were subsequently concerned with the heavy use of the collections. Whereas, only three faculties indicated that their second major reason for failure was that QUT did not hold the journal title. As one would expect, the Faculty of Science was one of these, as well as the Faculty of Built Environment and Engineering and the Faculty of Arts.

The major implication for the different categories of users is, that postgraduate and undergraduate students as well as academic staff fail primarily in their search for information due to QUT not holding the issue they require. Consequently, more extensive back runs of serials are considered a higher priority than additional titles. At the same time, a significant proportion of library patrons are failing due to heavy usage of existing collections.

How Do Libraries Apply Their Limited Acquisitions Dollars?

Do libraries cancel print indexes and abstracts when acquiring the CD-ROM service?

There are number of issues which need to be considered here. Firstly, print subscriptions provide multi-user access, whereas similar multi-user access to the CD-ROM services is often an expensive venture. Secondly, it is important to carefully study licence agreements. If the contract stipulates return of all compact disks, software and manuals upon cancellation of the service, then the library may well need to retain the print version. At the same time, often the CD-ROM service is available at a discount rate if the library subscribes to either the print version and/or the online database. Lastly, online access to current information is a priority whether considering cancelling print or CD-ROM indexes and abstracts. Online is also needed to supplement the usual three to four month lag in production before the next CD-ROM is available.

Should libraries cancel hard copy journals in favour of electronic journals?

> A full-text electronic periodical is a serial publication in machine readable form, delivered via computer to the user directly (as on CD-ROM) or over a telecommunications network, but not necessarily only available in electronic format.[6]

Therefore, in the context of this study, electronic journals are available via CD-ROMs services, online search services and the academic networks, where we are generally referring to AARNET and the INTERNET. There was overwhelming resistance from all categories of users surveyed to the proposition of cancelling print journals to help pay for the electronic services, such as full-text databases. While 73% disagreed with cancelling parallel print journals, 68% of the sample had indicated they would be likely to use full-text CD-ROM databases if they were available in their discipline. In other words library patrons would like both.

Again there is the question of access. Two hundred business students would have to book well in advance to use Business Periodicals OnDisk (BPO) if we cancelled all duplicate subscriptions. There is I believe an argument to cancel print versions of the more esoteric journals, but certainly not the core journals. One student's objection to the cancellation of print journals helps to remind librarians that library patrons approach their research in a variety of ways:

> Research students particularly need to *browse* through *real* journals using unstructured techniques to explore themes.

Valid concerns were also expressed by both science and information technology students with regard to electronic versions not necessarily replicating the diagrams and structures which are essential for these disciplines. Computer Select is one product where this is a problem.

In order to maintain expensive service, do libraries charge?

Libraries are becoming increasingly entrepreneurial in their approach to funding expensive services. Often faculty are lobbied for a contribution towards the initial installation of services such as BPO. Faculty may also be willing to transfer funds to the library to assist in purchasing the initial year or two of a subscription. Such funds are rarely recurrent and the library must plan to absorb future costs.

Many Australian libraries introduced charges for the usage of CD-ROM services in conjunction with the installation of a full-text CD-ROM service or an image product such as BPO. In the United States it is common to treat CD-ROM databases as value-added services and charge for their usage. Generally, I found in this survey that while users say they 'just love CD-ROM,' not surprisingly they do not want to pay. In a survey of CD-ROM usage conducted at Columbia University, a student responded as follows to the issue of payment for CD-ROM services:

> The beauty of this type of resource is that it allows more 'browsing' in disciplines and databases from which you would not necessarily be expecting results. This is only true because (a) it is VERY fast, (b) it is relatively easy and (c) it is FREE. If costs were higher in time, effort, or money, it would not be as effective in broadening the scope of academic searching.[7]

The question posed in the QUT survey to address payment for using CD-ROM services was based upon current practice:

> To what extent, if any, would paying 30¢ per page to print deter you from using full-text databases?

Over fifty percent (56.6%) of the population responded that such a charge would be likely to deter them. Approximately 30% indicated it would be of no concern. Analysing responses by category of user, surprisingly the greatest objection arose from academic staff (69.4%), whose printing costs are met by the faculty. Perhaps this was a philosophical objection to user pays. Of the postgraduates, 57.5% indicated that charges would be likely to deter them. While the poor undergraduates objected the least, although this was a significant proportion (56.2%).

I would attribute some of these negative responses to many users being unfamiliar with the benefits of a full-text CD-ROM product as a suitable database may not yet be available in their discipline.

*The importance of journal information
to different categories of users*

Over 90% of academic staff and postgraduate students indicated they always or often needed journal information for their study, research or work. Undergraduate responses ranged from 39.5% of first year students often requiring journal articles, to 87.8% for years 2-3, and 71.8% for years 4+. The last result is quite disturbing, as students in years 4 and higher are required to undertake a project report or are in an honours stream, and should not be in lesser need of journal information than earlier years (see Graph 4).

I was also interested in whether there were categories of users who indicated that they often need journal information, but who rarely or infrequently used indexes or abstracts in any format. This, along with the previous result would be an indicator of user education needs. So, using cross tabulations I found, firstly, that 132 respondents who indicated that they always or often required journal articles, used print indexes and abstracts infrequently or never. That is, 37% of the sample. Secondly, 144 of those sampled with the same need for journal articles had never or infrequently used CD-ROM databases. Therefore, close to 40% of the population are not familiar with the most popular and useful means of locating journal articles. Browsing is obviously a common method used for locating information, with some respondents relying heavily upon the new serials display.

From the collection development perspective it is important to identify if the need for back issues of journals is similar for all categories of users and similar across all faculties. Those surveyed

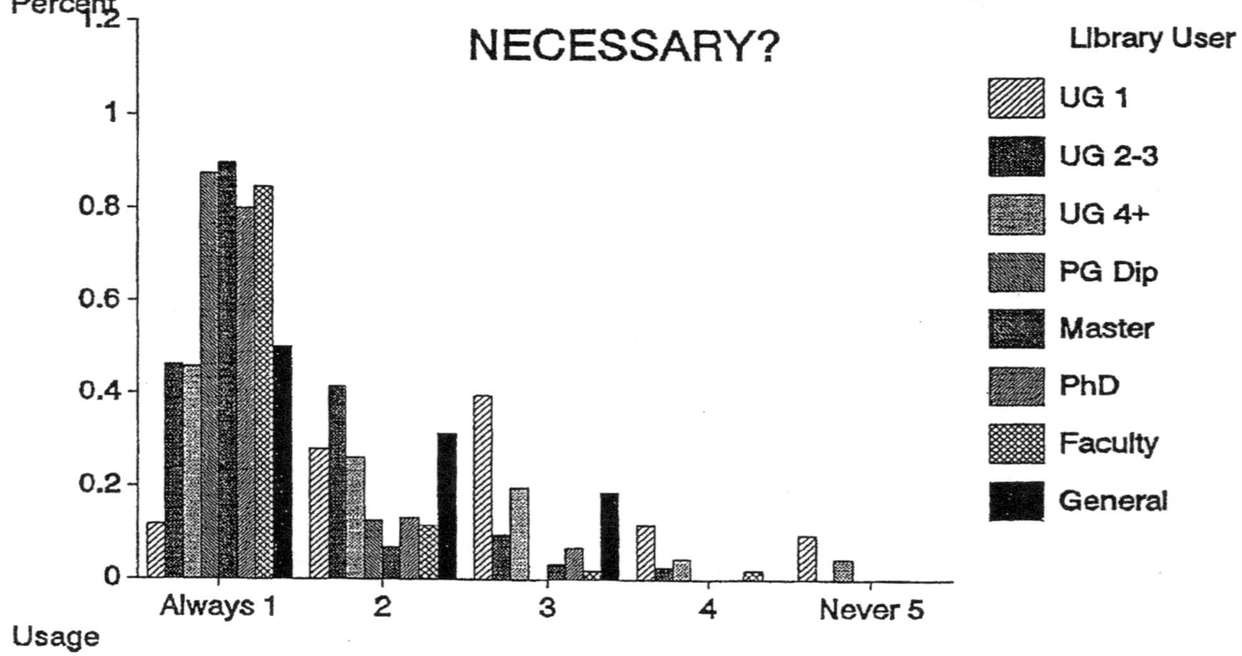

were asked to indicate whether they needed journal information published

   a. in the last 10 years
   b. from between 5 and 10 years ago
   c. earlier than 10 years.

For all categories of users (undergraduates, postgraduates, academic staff and general staff), the greatest demand is for journal articles published in the last 5 years. Over 90% of master students, doctoral students and academic staff need current journal information 'often.'

For journal articles published from 5 to 10 years ago, undergraduates require access to these back issues only sometimes. Whereas, over 50% of the postgraduate students and academic staff also need frequent access to these journal articles. It is primarily doctoral students (40%) who require access to journal information published more than 10 years ago. This was higher than the response for academic staff of 26%.

Now to consider faculty responses, all faculties indicated a high need for journal articles published in the last five years. A significant return of over 50% of the sample was received from the faculties of Arts, Education and Science for articles published between five and ten years ago. As would be anticipated, the greatest demand for journal articles published more than ten years ago was from the Faculty of Science. While all faculties indicated a need to consult pre-1982 journals from time to time, a very low response was received from the Faculty of Information Technology. Seventy-three percent indicated that they infrequently or never search for such older material.

Demand for Document Supply Services

The survey has already highlighted that most users require greater breadth to the collections, with the issues they require either not being held or not on the shelves. Concurrently, most of the demand is for journal articles published in the last ten years. Therefore, to what extent are users relying upon the library's document supply services?

Naturally, for faculties involved in cross campus teaching or where relevant resources are distributed due to their interdisciplinary nature, then high usage of *intercampus loan* services was evident. In particular, for the Faculties of Education, Arts and Business.

The *Special Reciprocal Loan Service* has proven to be the least patronised by all faculties. The Faculty of Education showed the heaviest usage at 22.2%, attributable to the holdings of the Mount Gravatt campus of Griffith University still displaying on QUT's library catalogue at the time the survey was conducted. The faculties relying most heavily on the *Interlibrary Loan Service* were, firstly, Science with 58.6% of the sample often requiring document supply of information not owned by QUT. Information Technology also indicated heavy usage (48.5%). For the latter, however, the need was for access to a wide range of current titles with little demand for back issues. Consequently, the pattern of demand for Information Technology was quite different in comparison to the other faculties. The Faculty of Education (38.1%) and the Faculty of Built Environment and Engineering (37.8%) have also been placing significant demands on the library's interlibrary loan services (see Graph 5).

IN SUMMARY, WHERE DOES THIS LEAD US?

I believe QUT is representative of university libraries in Australia and the Unites States, whereby the current level of acquisitions funding is not enabling libraries to purchase sufficient journal titles or expand holdings in terms of back issues, in order to meet the information needs of its clientele. As we have seen, this applies particularly to postgraduate students. In the case of QUT, especially staff and students in the Faculties of Science, Information Technology, Education and Built Environment and Engineering.

Consequently, libraries are relying heavily on their document supply services such as inter-library loans. It is also evident that such services will be unable to cope with projected growth. Therefore, we need to consider, firstly, whether there are alternative

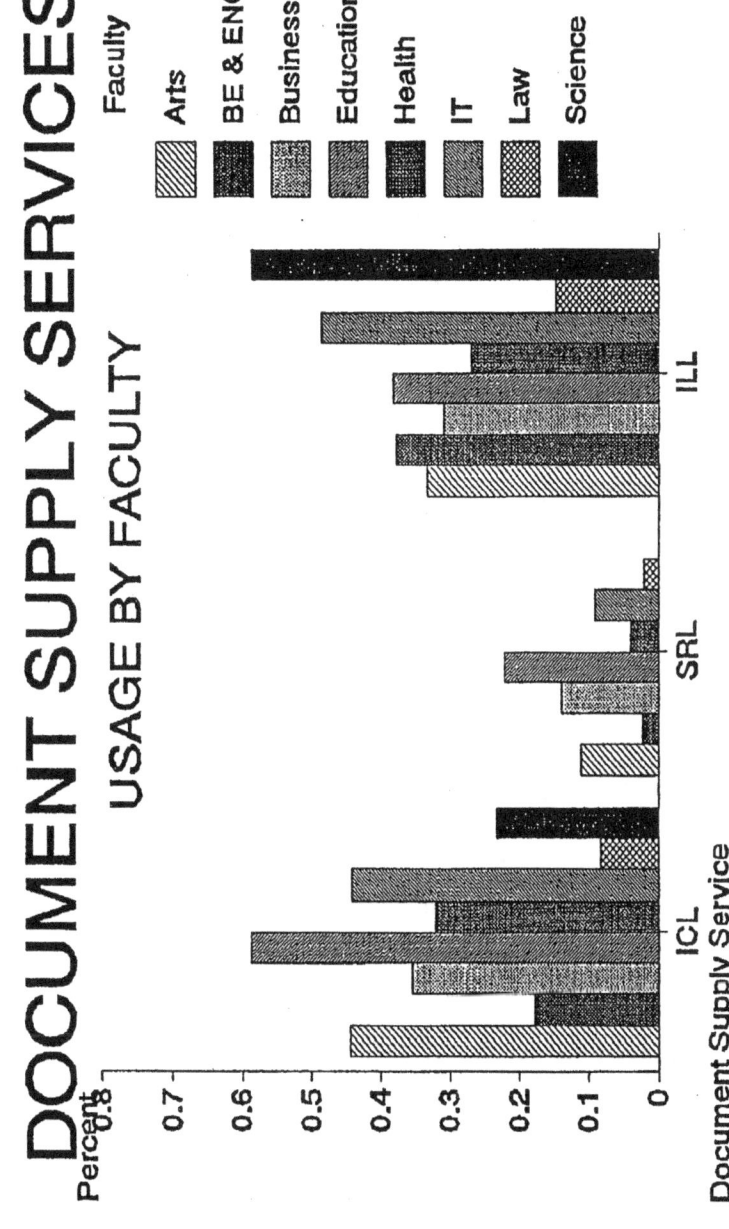

means of providing journal information. Secondly, what are the most cost effective solutions. The latter may take into account charging for value-added services, such as document supply services.

Alternative Means of Providing Journal Information

Some alternatives to be considered follow:
(i) Traditional serials suppliers are now branching into document supply. That is, the supply of a requested article as opposed to a journal title. Concerns with the erosion of market share due to such projects as ADONIS have assisted in this development.

(ii) In addition, electronic journals on the academic networks may provide alternative access to some journals, often with no subscription fee charged.

(iii) Tough questions need to be addressed, such as whether redistributing acquisitions dollars to document supply services would improve access to journal information required for research. This was commonly suggested by postgraduate students in this survey.

(iv) While I am referring to tough questions, it may be essential to pass the costs associated with the supply of documents onto the user in order to cope with the increases in demand.

(v) Lastly, there has been increased activity in Queensland in terms of regional cooperation with the establishment of the Brisbane University Libraries Office of Co-operation. Cooperative collection development strategies such as joint purchases of expensive services and rationalisation of specialist collections will no doubt be discussed in this forum.

The Impact of New Technologies

The development of more sophisticated means of identifying journal information through the application of computerised systems has been a significant factor in the demand for a greater breadth of journal titles as well as collection depth.

Users are attracted to electronic means of locating journal information, such as via CD-ROMs and online search services. And yet, libraries are restricted in their ability to rationalise duplicate services due to (a) the problems associated with access and the expense of networking and (b) the cost structures often applied which encourage subscription to duplicate services.

Many libraries will not consider purchase of a CD-ROM service unless it is able to be networked at a reasonable cost. Within the context of access, it may become more attractive to mount journal article citation databases on local systems rather than become committed to extensive local area network development for the purposes of CD-ROM access. Particularly, as Australian libraries are generally moving to their next generation of library system either through replacement or upgrade strategies. This approach would address the 'pile-up at the reference desk' scenario where reference librarians need to instruct users on a variety of search engines.

While there is an attraction to searching for journal citations electronically, there is still resistance to the electronic journal, as well as resistance to cancelling the duplicate print journals. While 60% of QUT library patrons are familiar with the most effective means of locating journal information, many still rely upon browsing and new serials displays in their research. Contents page services, whether hard copy or electronic, would assist in meeting this need for browsing. Again, libraries may provide such services internally for journals they hold, or rely upon commercial services such as ISI's current contents or turn to serials suppliers to provide contents pages for journals the suppliers distribute, not only journals subscribed to by the library.

In summary, looking at a scenario of continuing low-growth budgets for libraries in the higher education sector, then the focus is definitely moving from ACQUISITION to ACCESS.

REFERENCES

1. Whitaker, Cathy S. "Pile-up at the reference desk: teaching users to use CD-ROMs" *Laserdisk Professional*, March 1990, pp. 30-34.

2. Applied Science and Technology Index, Business Periodicals Index, Library Literature, Index to Legal Periodicals, MLA International Bibliography and Art Index are also networked.

3. The four campuses which currently offer CD-ROM services were surveyed: Carseldine, Gardens Point, Kedron Park and Kelvin Grove. There is a small campus at Nambour, the Sunshine Coast campus, which provides no access to CD-ROMs at this stage.

4. Michalak, Joseph A. "Observations on the use of CD-ROM in academic libraries" in *The Serials Librarian,* Vol. 17, No. 3/4, 1990, pp. 63-67.

5. Responses to survey questions were generally on a scale of 1 to 5. When analysing the results it is important to account for the halo effect, whereby many will never select the extremes of 1 or 5.

6. Okerson, Ann. "Accessing electronic journals: a survey of Canadian and American Libraries" in *The Serials Librarian*, Vol. 15, No. 1/2, 1988, p. 74.

7. Juhl, B. and Lowry, A. "The CD-ROM 'revolution' at Columbia: year one" in *Serials Librarian*, Vol. 17, No. 3/4, 1990, p. 73.

The E-Journal: Experiences at the State Library of New South Wales

Janine Schmidt

The topic today is an exciting one, and I congratulate the organizers on their foresight in addressing it. It is nearly twenty years since Lancaster first prognosticated the paperless library. While none of us believes in "paperless" any more, the "Library without walls" concept is becoming a reality, and we are all faced with how we amalgamate electronic forms of information into our library services, no matter whom we are serving, or how large, or small, our Library is.

I note that many of the attendees at this seminar are from the academic sector or from Queensland, and as I have been asked to examine the state library sector, I shall first do a thumbnail sketch of the Library and its services, for those of you who may be unfamiliar with our downtown Sydney site and our aims and objectives. Then I shall look at what the E-Journal means to us, and how it is impacting both on service provision and collection management.

The building which still typifies what the State Library of New South Wales is to most Sydneysiders and indeed Australians, is the Mitchell Wing. The image presented is scholarly; its portals tend to be forbidding; the focus is Australiana and our users are largely academics, writers, and researchers of various persuasions, many of whom have used the Library for many years and have expectations of an in-depth reference and information service. The Macquarie Street wing, opened in 1988, presents an entirely different image. It is open and friendly; emphasizes easy access to information; houses the wide-ranging collections of the General Reference Library; provides newspaper and telephone inquiry services; contains a Legal

© 1992 by The Haworth Press, Inc. All rights reserved.

Information Access Centre; and the clients are business people, family historians, professionals seeking updating in their chosen careers, people problem solving in relation to their work, and students, who attracted by our pleasant spaces and friendly services are inundating us in ever-increasing numbers.

In short, the State Library of New South Wales is today in the information communication business and provides a wide variety of information products and services. It houses a collection of over 3,000,000 items valued in excess of 500,000,000 and ranging from heritage materials like first fleet diaries and colonial oil paintings to CD-ROMs and videodiscs. The services provided are also wide-ranging, including educational tours, exhibitions on topics as diverse as *Bligh* and *Sport in Australia*, business information services, special needs services and a family history service. The Library's services extend throughout New South Wales, serving clients directly from the Macquarie Street site, and indirectly through public and other libraries. The public library network extends through 89 libraries and over 300 branches. The Library employs a staff of 440, of whom 45 are paid from funds raised from non-government sources, and its 1991/92 budget is A$35,000,000 of which A$15,000,000 is distributed to local government public libraries in the form of grants and subsidies. While most of the State Library's core services are provided free of charge, a number of value-added services are fee-based. The Library has nine commercial activities, which include hire of the facilities, conservation and photographic services, a publications program, and consultancy services. We have an active Friends group known as the Library Society, which also provides us with a team of over 200 volunteers, and have established a Foundation which has raised a capital sum of A$4.1 million in just over 4 years. The Library's mission statement is *"We are creating for the community a thriving dynamic organisation, leading the NSW library system so that it becomes one of the world's best in collecting, conserving and communicating information."* A detailed corporate planning process sets the overall directions, with action plans for each branch of the Library. Our catchcries are *"From History to High Tech"* and *"From Anywhere in the World to Anywhere in the State."*

What technologies do we use at the State Library? Unlike many of you who may be part of a larger organisation, we provide our own hardware, and do not have available to us the large mainframes of many of the university libraries. A variety of hardware and software is used to provide a range of support services, as well as public services. The Library has moved fairly rapidly from a single on-line searcher in 1979 to trials with ISDN services and remote access in 1992. Our CD-ROM services have proved extremely popular with clients, although we have not yet solved all the problems of effective service delivery.

I have spent some time describing the Library, its services, and our vision, because these impact so heavily on our view of the E-Journal. What then is the E-Journal? We have heard a number of definitions today. The literature also presents a variety of perspectives. In thinking about this topic, and I suppose feeling nostalgic about coming to Queensland, I was reminded of my early school days, when at the age of 4 and a half, I can recall sitting at a small wooden desk with a slate in front of me in Sherwood Public School, in a class of 65 (you can count them in the school photograph), chanting "E's like an egg with a bit taken out–E says eh." For some, an E-Journal is like a journal with a bit taken out, that is, the paper. An E-Journal can then be defined as a journal without a print counterpart. That really begs the question in a sense of what is a print counterpart and where is it? Does it mean a journal that has not first been issued in print form? Does it mean a journal that is not received by a particular library in print form? Does an E-journal which has been printed out into paper form no longer constitute an E-journal? Does E-journal really refer to the means of creation and publication? And to go back to my school memories of what "E" is, is an E-journal a printed journal whose content has been scanned and a bit image produced, or one created or scanned in ASCII format only? Do informal newsletters, bulletin boards, electronic mail discussions constitute an E-journal? Do the single journal articles supplied now by suppliers like Faxon constitute part of the E-journal? And what is a journal anyway? The easy wisdom learnt in library school that a book or a monograph is a publication complete in itself when issued, with the possibility of further editions, again each complete in itself; and a journal is a publication which when first issued is intended to continue indefinitely has become very clouded by current electronic publishing and the use of word processing. For certain types of content, the book itself may well disappear. Or is that again one of those predictions that has been around for some time, but which will never come true? Is what we are talking about really the E-library rather than the E-journal?

The terms serial, periodical, journal, magazine, newspaper, newsletter, annual, proceedings, yearbook have all been used to refer to those publications which when first issued were intended to continue indefinitely, the various words being used to refer to frequency of publication, format and type of content. Something popular or of a general nature is usually called a magazine–something scholarly a journal or periodical. A newspaper is usually produced more frequently and on poorer quality paper. Newspapers and magazines have been considered to be more ephemeral. Serial has been the overall term adopted. Most of the discussion on E-journals focuses on what is usually called the periodical or journal, and the content has been primarily of a more scholarly nature, and reasonably specific in subject matter. While I agree that the future is with us, the literature on this topic is more guarded than much I have read in the last twenty years about what the immediate future presents.

However, for us at the State Library of New South Wales, the E-journal encompasses consideration of all of these types, as we seek to serve our clients. For us, the E-journal is:

- an electronic form of regularly issued publication whether available on disk (CD-ROM, floppy, etc.), tape, or accessed online, which
- may also be used in paper format
- is not limited to a specific user group and
- includes bulletin boards and online discussion groups.

Before leaving the topic of what is an E-journal, I would like to reflect on why journals exist at all. One of the first journals to appear was the Philosophical Transactions of the Royal Society in 1605. This publication was produced to record scientific evidence and to communicate various developments to its members. While journals initially were produced by professional societies, commercial publishers also began publishing journals. Journals are still published to record research, document ideas, communicate findings, educate and assist in knowledge transfer and growth–as well as the publish or perish syndrome, which ensures a steady stream of journal articles. The so-called popular magazines are published for similar reasons, with entertainment as a prime reason, and the profit motive more firmly in mind. People who write journal articles do so for reasons which are different from those who read. The needs of those who write may well be met by E-journals, but it is questionable whether all the needs of readers will be met by this medium. While keeping up with one's own immediate field of expertise via an E-journal is comparatively easy, browsing related areas electronically is difficult. The computerized current awareness services available for some time have proved useful in circumstances where needs can be clearly defined. The same will probably occur with E-journals.

Having examined how we define E-journals at the State Library of New South Wales, what then are we doing about them? When CD-ROM services first became available, the Library purchased many indexing services considered relevant–by our definition E-journals. The State Library was extremely interested in *Business Periodicals Ondisc* when it first came on to the market. The amount of money allocated by the State government to expenditure on materials for the Library's collections has not over the last fifteen years in any way kept up with inflation, let alone the increases in publishing output. The increase in serials publication in the business area has taken place over this time scale, and our collection was woefully inadequate. Acquisition of BPO was seen as an immediate means of rectifying this problem. An initial check established that one-third only of the titles listed in BPO was held by the State Library in full text. We therefore proceeded with the purchase, being the first library in Australia to do so. The service provided extremely popular with clients, who happily paid 30¢ per page to print out articles full text. We have since acquired *General Periodicals Ondisc* and *Social Sciences Index/Full Text*, and also hold *Computer Select*. We have now commenced cancellations of some serials held in hard copy, when these are also held on disc.

While our experience with E-journals has primarily been with the CD-ROM services available, some of our staff have been accessing some E-journals in the U.S. via ILANET and BITNET. In particular, the *Newsletter on Serials Pricing Issues* is regularly downloaded, taking 10-15 minutes per month to capture the file. Marcia Tuttle's experiences with the production of this journal are outlined in a recent issue of *Advances in Serials Management*, clearly delineating many of the problems associated with the production of E-journals. To print out a downloaded file takes time, as does also the redirection to recipients.

The State Library has experienced difficulties joining AARNet, and the cost of $30,000 per year for high data transfer access is considerable. We have therefore been unable as yet to access E-journals on both AARNet and the INTERNET. This highlights the difficulties of access to information available only on closed networks, and the very real challenge facing us is how to make this information available to the clients of the Library. The recently published *Directory of Electronic Journals* lists 30 journals and 60 newsletters. This is only the tip of the iceberg. The format is being produced totally outside the biographical control chain, and finding out what is being produced is extremely difficult. At the moment, it is clear that the subject matter of E-journals is reasonably specific and predominantly scholarly in nature, e.g., *Tetrahedron Computing Methodology, Journal of the Astronomical Society of the Atlantic.*

The E-journal is therefore making a limited impact on the general public. However, this situation is likely to change as more academic and professional communication occurs in electronic form.

Previous papers at this seminar have addressed economic issues. I confess to not fully understanding economics, but I do understand costs. I'm rather like Charles Dickens' Mr. Micawber "Annual income twenty pounds, annual expenditure nineteen nineteen and six, result happiness. Annual income twenty pounds, annual expenditure twenty pounds nought and six, result misery." As far as the Library's budget is concerned, result happiness is what we are looking for, and value for money. Our decision to focus on CD-ROM versions of journal titles is because we believe they save us money, and provide better value for our users.

Firstly, our own costs. We have not done an exact comparison of costs of the full text CD-ROM version, and the printed version of a journal, but we have looked at the total costs of BPO. We are paying an average of $67.57 per annum for each journal title. This excludes the cost of the index itself. The average price of journals in business and economics is given in the *Bowker Annual* for 1990 as $84.33. It appears therefore as if we are ahead on subscription prices. On top of that are the costs of handling, including accessioning, claiming, payment of individual invoices, end-processing, as well as binding and storage. These costs vary considerably from library to library, but if we estimate the costs to be somewhere between $50 and $100 per annum, then the savings on the CD-ROM version would be between $18,500 and $37,000. The State Library of New South Wales has a closed stack. Purchase of the CD-ROM version therefore also saves considerably on retrieval costs. One of the costs we have also reduced is cataloguing. An entry has been put on to the Library's Computer Catalogue for each title held on CD-ROM, including details of holdings and the fact that the title is held on CD-ROM. No subject headings are allocated, but an entry is made on ABN.

It is more difficult to measure the costs and value for our clients. Most of the costs incurred by users in accessing the Library's resources are associated with time and ease of use, and anything that can be done to reduce access times will reduce the costs. While the users of academic libraries, i.e., students, are frequently rich in the time and poor in financial resources, the users of libraries like the State Library of New South Wales are usually poor in terms of time, and relatively well off in financial terms. For them time is money. Since adding the titles held on CD-ROM to the Computer Catalogue, clients have been found to prefer the CD-ROM version, even when the hard copy is also held, because it is faster and easier to use. In looking at costs to users, there are significant savings in the use of CD-ROM journals for obtaining articles in terms of reduced time and ease in access and copying.

With access to E-journals, the direct user cost or cash paid may go up slightly, but the savings in time and effort appear to be valued more highly by many clients. There are however user costs, as well as library costs. The work stations required to access materials are expensive, and in a library one is not enough. With electronic formats, there is a substantial change in the roles of each participant in the information chain–author, publisher, bookseller or agent, library, and a redistribution of the costs. Printed book publishing is cost intensive at the creation side, and comparatively cheap at the user purchaser end. Electronic publishing may be cheaper at the production end of the equation (although on this point, the literature states that costs are similar), but more expensive at the user end in terms of the equipment required. Many electronic publishers are also discovering a considerable change in their role in terms of customer support. No-one ever asked a publisher how to read or use a printed journal, but publishers of electronic journals are experiencing a steady stream of customers seeking technical support in relation to both hardware and software. The costs of publication of most printed journals are met by advertising as well as subscription. With popular magazines, the advertising revenue far outstrips cover price income, constituting about 75%. Even with scholarly journals, the advertising revenue can be about 7.5%. Until advertising revenue is recovered in some way through electronic means as well, the production of E-journals will be inhibited. The wide disparity in prices for electronic products makes it clear that publishers are finding it difficult to determine appropriate prices for electronic products, particularly where print versions are also available. The purchaser of a print product pays once at the point of acquisition. It can then be read or used many times. An electronic product frequently incurs charges for each use. The future impact of these costs on both libraries and users is difficult to determine.

Digitized storage of journal articles will facilitate remote access by clients throughout New South Wales who will be able to search for required material remotely, and then have it transmitted using ISDN, or systems like ARIEL.

The journals which exist only on somebody's computer somewhere do present additional challenges for users. The practicalities of accessing, let alone, controlling the seemingly chaotic chunks of data swirling around in the electronic ether are significant. There are still difficulties in physical access to electronic formats, although local data, and indeed wide area networks can help, with access able to be distributed. The practical difficulties of network membership have already been mentioned. Few, if any, E-journals are indexed in the traditional indexing services. These journals are currently created outside the traditional refereeing systems–the old "garbage in garbage out" may well result, giving rise to questions of quality of the information.

There are other concerns with E-journals. Once downloaded, a document can be manipulated and altered in ways which may reflect on the integrity of the original item. There is also the presentation used. Most of the E-journals currently available on the academic networks are in ASCII format, bypassing the sophistication of five hundred years of printing. While improvements in electronic publishing will no doubt improve the presentation, it currently presents difficulties for satisfactory use. Preservation concerns are primarily those of libraries. The current policy of ACLIS on the preservation of machine-readable records is that a copy should be printed out. But whose responsibility is it to provide a copy for archival purposes? Our experience with newspapers at the State Library of New South Wales indicates that the publisher is uninterested in preservation copies, and the same may occur with E-journals. Libraries have traditionally ensured that a copy of an item survives, and will need to develop policies in this area. As more and more information becomes stored in electronic form, the problems of retrieval become more significant. Current interfaces are complex, and librarians must work to provide appropriate access to these information stores for their users.

In conclusion, the 1986 words of Katzen still apply.

> New techniques and technologies are introduced within an already existing context, social, economic, and intellectual, within which has developed a nexus of institutional and organizational structure, social roles, and norms. . . .

Some new technologies offer the possibility of improving existing ways of doing things. Others, which may be regarded as genuine new media, make it possible to do what could not be done or even envisaged before. A new medium is more likely to lead to a new distribution of functions between different media rather than to the total displacement or elimination of the old by the new.

The E-journal will solve old problems and create new ones. The E-journal will succeed if it meets the needs of both writers and readers. E-journals will both assist in the client services and collection management and present new challenges. Libraries will amalgamate this format into their services as they have amalgamated every additional improvement of format since the clay tablet–and the changes will be evolutionary, rather than revolutionary.

REFERENCES

BUTLER, B. "The electronic library program: developing networked electronic library collections," *Library High Tech* vol. 9 issue 34 pp21-30 (1991).

CLACK, M.E., McMILLAN, Gail and others. "Electronic journals: consideration for the present and the future," *Serials Review* vol. 17 no. 4 pp 77-86 (Winter 1991).

COLLINS, Tim. "Electronic publishing: the publisher's perspective," *CD-ROM Librarian* vol. 6 pp12-15 (1991).

FECKO, M.B. and LANGSCHIED, L. "The impact of electronic journals in traditional library services," *Serials Librarian* vol. 21 nos. 2/3 pp185-187 (1991).

KATZEN, May. "Electronic publishing in the humanities," *Scholarly Publishing* vol. 18. pp5-16 (Oct. 1986).

KING, Timothy B. "The impact of electronic and networking technologies on the delivery of scholarly information," *Serials Librarian* vol. 21 nos. 2/3 pp5-13 (1991).

KURZWEIL, Raymond. "The future of libraries. Part 1. The technology of the book," *Library Journal* vol. 117 no. 1 pp80-82 (Jan. 1992).

LANCASTER, F.W. *Towards paperless information systems* (London: Academic Press, 1978).

LANGSCHIELD, Linden. "The changing shape of the electronic journal," *Serials Review* vol. 17 no. 3 pp7-14 (1991).

LOWRY, C.B. "Information technologies and the transformation of libraries and librarianship," *Serials Librarian* vol. 21 nos. 2/3 pp109-132 (1991).

NIELSEN, Brian. "The Coalition For Networked Information: Realizing The Virtual Library," *Online* vol. 15 pp96-97 (Sept. 1991).

PITERNICK, Anne B. "Electronic serials: realistic or unrealistic solution to the journal crises?" *Serials Librarian* vol. 21 nos. 2/3 pp15-31 (1991).

SMITH, E. "The Print Prison," *Library Journal* vol. 117 no. 2 pp48-51 (1 Feb. 1992).

TUTTLE, M. "The newsletter on serials pricing issues: teetering on the cutting edge," *Advances in Serial Management* vol. 4 pp37-63 (1992).

The View from the Other Side of the Disc

Julie Stevens

1. WHY ME?

I have now been a library consultant at ALDIS for two years and in that time have been actively participating in the introduction of image databases on a large scale to Australian libraries. Previously, I have been employed as a researcher at the Australian Bureau of Statistics, Canberra, looking at the provision of information in different formats, and in different media. I have formal qualifications in both information management and marketing.

This paper draws on my experience with the installation of 32 image databases on many different sites and my contact with many serials librarians, administrators, cataloguers, acquisitions staff, technical support people and others who support library staff in their day-to-day, and budget-to-budget activities.

2. ALDIS PTY LTD

Formed in 1986, ALDIS is an associate company of CLSI Australia, a major supplier of computer-based library systems and services. ALDIS has built on the experience which CLSI has developed through the years of service to the Australian library community. With CLSI, ALDIS shares a total commitment to library automation and the information services field.

ALDIS distributes over 80 CD-ROM database titles from the

© 1992 by The Haworth Press, Inc. All rights reserved.

world's leading CD-ROM publisher, SilverPlatter, as well as from UMI, The Library Corporation, INFORMIT, and Longman/Microinfo. Leading the field, ALDIS introduced CD-ROM to Australian libraries in 1986 with "Bibliofile" from the Library Corporation.

We don't just distribute however. Development of computer-based library products is a priority at ALDIS. ALDIS has researched the "Gravity" Downline loading package for use with ABN, and also "Levity," our PC-based ABN terminal cluster for ABN users.

We also develop, integrate, and support complete CD-ROM network solutions, helping libraries make greatest use of their existing facilities whether they be databases, software applications, hardware or even existing networks.

But most importantly, customer support is ALDIS' top priority. Comprehensive technical, hardware and software support is guaranteed with every product bought from ALDIS.

3. THE ISSUE AT HAND: IMAGE DATABASES

When CD-ROM databases were introduced, they revolutionized the way we search for information. CD-ROM technology combined the best of many world's. . . . the convenience of paper-copy indexes. . . . the power of online searching. . . . the predictable cost of annual subscription products.

Abstract-and-index databases have already been available for some time, now organisations such as UMI have taken ondisc access one step further with full text image databases.

Now you don't even have to leave the workstation to get the full text of articles you need. You can use an image database instead and get exact article copies from the system's laser printer, or just view the articles themselves on the computer's screen.

I'd like just to briefly explain how UMI's image databases work, because I think that this may help clarify a few of the issues I raise a little later regarding the impact of this new technology.

4. IMAGE DATA BASES: HOW THEY WORK

Searching by keyword etc.:

	INDEX COMPONENT
Search term:	Keyword, author, title etc. ↓
Retrieves:	Relevant Citations ↓
Displays/Prints:	Abstract ↓
	IMAGE COMPONENT ↓
Displays/Prints:	Image Replica of articles

Searching by periodical:

	IMAGE COMPONENT ↓
Select:	Publication title ↓
Select:	Relevant Issue ↓
Display/Print:	Image replica of issue/article

5. THE IMPACT OF THE ISSUE

As you can probably imagine, every information seeker's eyes light up at the prospect of the "easy life" these image databases suggest. And they are easy to use. They do make article retrieval one of the lesser problems of the researcher rather than one of the greater. The user doesn't even have to ask the librarian where the appropriate shelving is, let alone tracking missing issues down. But this is all from the user's perspective. What about the librarian?

In our experience of installing 32 image databases, there have been a number of recurrent questions that are asked of us by library staff. In most cases these questions have been simple to answer, in a number a little more effort was required. For a few, there are still no complete solutions, but rest assured we're working on these. I'd like to raise some of these issues, and provide some answers today.

5.1 Funding: Where Does the Money Come From?

Almost every information provider would agree that to have an image database installed in their library would improve their ability to serve their clientele. Not every library has the funds available to make this happen.

Some libraries, however, are able to raise the funds–as evidenced by the 32 UMI image databases sites currently established in Australia and New Zealand.

What methods have they employed to raise these funds?

Obviously I can't go through all of the possibilities, however a couple of scenarios are as follows:

a. Some libraries seem to have raised funds through the award of grants by the Commonwealth Government.
b. Others have cancelled print journal subscriptions to pay the invoice involved.
c. A couple of academic libraries have lobbied the relevant schools or departments on campus in an attempt to raise funds. For example, by obtaining an agreement from the School of Business that if the school purchases the hardware required to run an image database system, the library will pay subscription costs to BPO for the following 3 years.

So although costs may look prohibitive at first, there are ways around the problem.

5.2 Cost Recovery–or Can We Charge for Copies?

Once an image database system is installed, this system may be used to recover some of the costs incurred.

For example, with UMI's range of image databases it is possible to attach a debit card mechanism such as a Resource Card or Copytex unit to the laser printer and charge a certain value for each image print made from the system.

Originally, UMI introduced this facility to enable libraries to re-coup royalty payments from users, but this also provides the facility for libraries to reclaim costs of consumables, staff time, etc. UMI's policy on cost recovery is that as long as the established charges are "reasonable" they have no objection.

5.3 Royalties–the Publisher's Cut

Those of you who have been aware of UMI's range of image databases for some time will probably also have been aware that UMI placed a "royalty" fee on each image print made from the system. This royalty amount was recorded by the system, and downloaded to a floppy disk by the library on a monthly basis as part of the update process. The floppy disk would then be returned to UMI, and the library invoiced, via ALDIS, on a quarterly basis. UMI would then decode the information on the royalty disk and distribute the funds collected to the publishers.

As of January 1, 1992 this royalty fee was discontinued for Australian/New Zealand customers. Effectively the royalties have been absorbed by the subscription cost, and UMI have given an assurance that these subscription costs will not rise in the short term. It is still necessary to collect the royalty data, and return the disk to UMI however, so that UMI may distribute funds to publishers as appropriate.

At least with the removal of the royalty fee, there's one less issue for library staff to be concerned about.

5.4 Copyright–Reproduction of Articles

At the bottom of every image page printed from a UMI full text workstation are the sentences:

> Reproduced with permission of copyright owner. Further reproduction prohibited.

These sentences are designed to advise the user that he or she is not permitted to make photocopies of output from the system. Originally, of course, this extra copying would have served to by-pass conditions where the copying is within copyright law. All copies made would need to be recorded in a way that allows UMI to make the royalty payments to publishers. This is one of those issues that is on its way to being resolved.

5.5 Hardware Supply and Support–Down-Time

Like any computer system, image database hardware can have its problems. Monitors can suffer in buildings with faulty power supplies, computers can get damaged by both computer literate and illiterate users. All of these problems are issues that can cause a nervous librarian to panic–should the faulty equipment get that far.

All hardware systems supplied by ALDIS are configured and tested before dispatch, so that any of the manufacturer's defects can be ironed out before the library even knows there was potential for a problem to occur.

The majority of our systems are also installed by trained ALDIS personnel, so that any site specific problems can be discussed at the time of installation. (Would you know whether to put the tower CPU on the floor or the desk?)

And if there is a problem in the field a return to base warranty service is provided free of charge for the first 12 months, and by contract after that period. Most sites are reached on an overnight basis, with swap-out of equipment, so that the least possible "down-time" occurs.

5.6 Software Support–or HELP! A Student
Just Deleted all the Files from the Hard Disk

Believe it or not, it is possible to solve by far the majority of software problems over the phone.

Because the type of image database systems we're discussing run on IBM compatible machines running MS DOS, even such a problem as a student deleting all files from the hard disk can be solved very quickly over the phone. The installation process is actually quite simple–remember, most data are stored on CD-ROM, not on the computer–and with a bit of helpful advice, an instruction sheet and software in hand, the librarian should have no major problems getting a system up and running again in only an hour or two.

As for inconsistencies and irregularities ... with 32 sites it's not very often we haven't seen the problem before, and have found the cause and solution. The worst you may have to do is re-install software to copy over a corrupt file.

Librarians don't need to be computer experts to support their image database systems, as long as they know where to go for help.

5.7 Administration: The "What If?" and "How Do We?" Questions

There are a number of administrative issues that cause librarians some concern when they're thinking about full text systems. For example:

Security

One of the frequently asked questions is "What happens if a user steals a disk?"

If a disk goes missing from your collection, or if one gets damaged, UMI will replace that disk free of charge. In most cases this is an overnight service from our Melbourne office.

If the whole set of, say, 400 BPO disks just "disappears" then there is likely to be a negotiable replacement cost involved. After all, that's a cabinet measuring 3 feet by 2 feet by 2 feet that just walked out the door. Which leads me to ...

Fire and Other Unthinkable Disasters

Interestingly enough, the only organisation that has ever asked what would happen in case of fire is the only one to have had a fire! Luckily there wasn't much damage in this case.

We recommend that the library insure its image database equipment like all other major resources.

Cataloguing

To catalogue or not to catalogue? This is a major issue facing many libraries. Most librarians are choosing to catalogue the individual journal titles as part of their collection, for the same reasons as they would otherwise catalogue the hard copy. And speaking of hard copy...

Retention of Hard Copy Journals

There is no easy answer as to whether a library should keep its hard copy journal collections after purchasing those titles as part of an image database. There are obvious advantages to having the hard copy, e.g., multi-user access, circulation, shelf browsers.

There are also obvious disadvantages: cost, processing, missing issue location, storage.

All that can be said is that from our experience some libraries do, some libraries don't.

Ownership/Leasing of Disks

A major concern of potential purchasers/users of image database systems is that they may be required to return the image disks should they cancel their database subscription, thereby losing their copies of the journals for the subscription period if they have cancelled hard copy.

UMI's policy is that if the subscription is held for 3 years the disks may be kept by the subscriber with the condition that they must continue to return the royalty information to UMI for forwarding to the publisher.

6. IN CONCLUSION

In conclusion then, I've covered a number of the frequently asked questions regarding image database systems, and I hope that this has resolved a few of the issues raised today also.

I've looked at (if very briefly) some of the monetary problems, legal issues, support problems, and even a few general, administrative difficulties faced by sites taking on image database systems. These are all problems being faced now. I'd like to finish with some news for the future however.

The next major release in these imaging systems will be networking. As you can well imagine, the most important component in the success of this scenario is a large capacity, reliable, working jukebox. ALDIS, in conjunction with UMI, will be progressively releasing details of networking options in the next twelve months. At the ALIA conference in September/October 1992, we will be demonstrating such a system. By this time in 1993, we anticipate having a working reference site.

Cyberspace Economics

Don Lamberton

I might begin by mentioning that I wear several hats:

(a) I am an editor of both a domestic Australian and a foreign journal–*Prometheus* and *Information Economics and Policy*, plus being an active member of some other editorial boards *Telecommunications Policy, Economics of Innovation and New Technology, Futures Research Quarterly* and *TDF Report*;

(b) I am a user of journals, both within economics and information science and over a range of interdisciplinary interests;

(c) I have had a role in what I might call simply 'the library world'; and

(d) I have been long concerned with the application of economics to all matters of information and knowledge, i.e., what has been allowed, rather grudgingly, to become recognized as information economics.

Out of this mix of interests I was led to select the title: *Cyberspace Economics*. Why not just *Information Economics* as it appeared in the preliminary version of the seminar programme? After all, I have often argued that economics has to be information economics in this Information Age. The *Cyberspace* version grew out of reviewing Michael Benedikt's MIT Press book of that title for *Prometheus*. The terms, coined by William Gibson in his 1984 novel *Neuromancer*, applies to "an infinite artificial world where humans navigate in information-based space"–the ultimate human-computer interface–a world behind the computer screen as magical and marvelous as the one Alice discovered behind her looking glass. According to the blurb, cyberspace is both the strangest and most radically innovative of today's computer developments.

Because the world's economies have been gorging themselves on computer technology and we have had so much difficulty detecting

© 1992 by The Haworth Press, Inc. All rights reserved.

the enormous productivity gains that technology was supposed to bring (without causing unemployment), I allowed myself to be persuaded by the sub-title, *First Steps*, to do a review in the hope of some glimpses of this brave new wired world. It had obvious economic implications and was relevant to *The Electronic Journal*, for in cyberspace everyone, or so it seemed at first, would be able to access the "vast data bases that constitute the culture's deposited wealth, every document is available, every recording is playable, and every picture is viewable" (Benedikt, p. 2).

Economic constraints seem in this world to have been assumed away, although not entirely so as some everyday features of our economic life are still present. There are cyber-sweatshops where workers act within a severely restricted and sensually impoverished world; the cyberspace corporation needs start-up capital; a worker has some property rights in his or her PVW (Personal Virtual Workspace); the public face of the corporation is still all-important and its personnel problems complex. These everyday features aside, one might wonder at the assumed capability of handling such a massive stock of information. In the environmental debate there are those who point to the state of London streets had that city persisted with its horse-drawn mode of transportation; but the street problem pales into insignificance compared with a globe denuded of trees and swathed in layers of scientific journals—not to mention *Picture* and *People*. Fortunately, cyberspace exists only in science fiction and the imagination of a few thousand people. While it is doubtful that it ever will exist, at least in the shape given it in current writings, technological and economic pressures and cyberspace thinking will together ensure that the future differs greatly from the past. Their interactions contribute to our knowledge and so to the patterns of economic development and institutional change.

Despite the assumed absence of immediate resource pressures, Benedikt's contributors—drawn from computer science, architecture, the visual arts, philosophy, anthropology and industry but not from economics—speculate about features that might prove to be very important in economic terms; for example, the way people adapt to the use of the computer. In this virtual reality created by computers with interactive software, people would not rely upon keyboards: they can also use voice, finger pointing, head nodding.

And the machine responds through wrap-around screens, video goggles, synthesizers, data gloves and anything else that can add to three-dimensional sense and sensation. Last year *The Australian* newspaper's Computers & High Technology section featured an article, "Safe 'silicone' sex is a virtual reality," which reported the availability of technology enabling people to hook themselves up to a virtual reality program, select a "partner"–Madonna or Julia Roberts were suggested–and engage in computer-simulated sex. Of course, pornography has already proved a money-spinner for French and other telecommunications systems. Perhaps such applications of what Thomas Bass calls electronic LSD "may be exactly what will break the ice between shy computers and people" (p. 30), with important implications, not necessarily all favourable, for economic development.

Economic development is both a generally accepted policy objective and a contentious definitional problem. I take it to mean "the creation of increasingly more complex structures of the division of labour" (Lei jonhufvud, p. 167). Historically, one might see reduced transport costs as the driving force in that development, with that role now shifting to the reduction of information costs: the costs of gathering, processing, storing, transmitting and using information. Taken together these costs are now the dominant resource-using activity in developed economies (Eliasson, p. 17).

Look more closely at these economic aspects of information activities. First, there is a much increased specialization in information occupations in libraries and computer firms, in industry and government. Just look at the job ads. Such specialization could well have become the most fundamental form of the division of labour. Second, the market form of organization that we tend to think of as the dominant form has had to adapt to this greater emphasis on information flows and information resources. True, information itself is traded more widely and information-related services of many kinds are a growing share of market transactions. However, information as a commodity has some definite limitations; it is indivisible and its benefits are difficult to appropriate. These fundamental characteristics combine with the capital nature of the expenditures on information, the control objectives that are usually present and imperfections of the legal system, to dictate internalization of information processes. They are thought best done within the boundaries of the organization. However, the complexity of the linkages between organizations and the prevailing uncertainty mean that the organization is an incompletely connected network of information flows. The boundaries are blurred and even the form of internal organization tends to undergo change. Some recent discussion has sought to emphasize the (business) intelligence role and stress that R&D, for example, is only a part, possibly a small part, of the on-going exploratory activity (Lamberton, 1992).

I have tried to sketch some of the basic features of the setting in which the scientific enterprise is conducted. We are confronted with the "unavoidable economic dimension. Economic factors shape and condition our cognitive proceedings in so fundamental a way that they demand explicit attention . . . [O]nly by heeding the concrete processes that engender our knowledge in a way that takes account of their economic dimension can we adequately explain the nature of its operations and properly understand the character of its products" (Rescher, p. 150). We encounter "the inescapable realities of resource limitations" (Rescher, p. 149). "The limits of science are very real, but they are not inherently intellectual matters of human incapacity or deficient brain power. They are fundamentally economic limits imposed by the technological character of our access to the phenomena of nature. The over-optimistic idea that we can push science ever onward to the solution of all questions that arise shatters in the awkward reality that the price of problem solving inexorably increases to a point beyond the limits of affordability" (Rescher, p. 150).

Given the resource and cost limitations, it may seem natural enough to entertain technological hopes and engage in somewhat naive forecasting, such as is involved in cyberspace. I shall turn in a moment or two to the electronic journal forecasts, but first let me comment on what I call 'roadblock' thinking.

The expectations reflected in these forecasts tend to produce a dangerous response. In the research community, there is a growing awareness of the human and organizational, i.e., non-technological, aspects of the new technologies; of the gap between the quite fantastic potential thought to be there and our rather limited capability for putting all the gadgets to effective use while things are organized the way they are–our universities with labs, faculties, interdisciplinary centres, and administrative arrangements; our industrial firms with their labs, profit centres and marketing divisions; our governmental organization in its centralized and decentralized forms.

The reality is one in which constraints may well be modified and relaxed so long as we see this clearly as an objective and recognize that we have to learn how to deal with these problems. These problems are themselves worthy of attention as research. Their solution requires that we invent new forms of organization rather than more machines, that we modify features of our society that are long established and highly valued. The pay-off from trying to move ahead in this way could be great. We must, however, avoid becoming "fixated on some technological utopia" and being so determined to get there that we see the constraints as "merely a collection of unforeseen roadblocks . . . requiring removal if the computer revolution is to proceed" (David and Steinmueller, p. 39). It is my judgement that the central issue here is my recognition that the scientific enterprise is essentially the production *and* utilization of information. It follows that we must adopt an information-theoretic approach: because research (and invention) are directed to producing information and its utilization calls for information flows, communication, and their management, "an economic analysis of R&D activities must inevitably rest upon recognition of the peculiar characteristics of information viewed as an economic commodity" (Dasgupta and David, p. 520).

Scientific journals of either the old-fashioned printed kind or the new electronic kind are part of this activity. What technological future has been predicted? Put simply, it is obsolescence for the old-fashioned printed journal. But please note that the predictions of the 1970s tend to still be the predictions of the 1990s. For Senders writing in the mid-1970s the electronic alternative was "almost inevitable given the joint pressures of volume of scientific material and the cost of traditional ways of doing things. It would be wise for all scientific investigators to act now to influence and support these new systems and to shape them according to what they believe to be best for the journals of the future" (Senders, p. 260). Compare this with Colin Steele in the 1990s: "The new age of electronic journals, "scholarly sky writing" and global data networks with "information superhighways" linking academics around the world is tailor-made for libraries struggling to be innovative and entrepreneurial in providing access to information for staff and students" (p. 23). He identifies problem issues, adding that "Electronic solutions *may be* the only way to tackle these issues" (Emphasis added). There is doubt because, for example, the new technologies have made it possible for libraries to hoard even more than before.

Of course, the slowness of these developments is a characteristic feature of technological change. Few if any of the technological developments of the next 20 years are not on hand today. Communications satellites were shown to be possible by Arthur Clarke's paper in *Wireless World* in 1945 and first went into operation in the 1960s. Packet switched networks and optical fibres have been around for 15 or more years. Even US high-tech weaponry during the Gulf War is said to have been 20-year old technology. So the World Brain is not lurking just around the corner. Even when new developments have been introduced their diffusion can be slow. Technology-push marketing of telecommunications might easily give the impression of a world with a phone in every home; in fact, half the world's population is not yet within two hours walking distance of a telephone (Butler). So much for the global village!

What were the faults of the old printed journal system? I suppose these could be traced to the inadequacies of the postal system and printing technology and to overworked editors. Together these pushed up costs. But there were other factors. Attempts to speed up the process tended to push up costs. So too did the increased fragmentation of research and the work specialization that it brought. There were more and more journals catering for smaller and smaller specialist groups. In this the scientists were aided and abetted by the publishers.

On an optimistic view, the new technology can cut through the delays, widen access, and lower costs. It would be wise to look carefully at the accounting. Let me give an illustration from Sender's paper.

OLD SYSTEM: "The article is mailed to the editor who puts it at the bottom of the pile of papers awaiting his attention. Eventually, when he gets around to reading the title and the abstract (and possibly the whole text), he chooses an associate editor, or one of his referees, and mails it off to him. The referee may or may not agree to deal with the particular article. Let us assume that he does. He then has to find time to read and review it. These are difficult and time-consuming processes" (pp. 257-8).

NEW SYSTEM: "Having selected the editor, [the author] puts the tape in the tape reader, types in the name of the editor ... The title, abstract, and other useful information appear that day, or three minutes after midnight, or whenever, on the editor's display. In the morning when the editor comes in, *he sees all the information there* ... [H]e may then choose an associate editor, or two or three" (Emphasis added. p. 258).

We are told there has been a quick gain of three or four weeks. But we are not told why the editor deals immediately with the article and now relies on the abstract. Nor is the involvement of extra referees costed. Given set-up costs for the electronic journal, it is not clear that costs are reduced, even if time is cut. I suspect the second scenario has been shaped by enthusiasm for adoption of the new system (a common circumstance) and the quality control that had been a feature of the old system may have suffered. I wish merely to suggest that the evaluation has to be done very carefully: there are systematic biases and a wide array of simplifying assumptions. The most common errors are:

1. underestimating the time need to achieve effective functioning of innovation, often by a considerable margin;
2. overestimating the average utilization rate as a basis for appraising benefits;
3. underestimating the need to make adaptive adjustments in the preceding and subsequent steps of an integrated ... operation; and
4. underestimating the problems and costs of gaining ... acceptance of associated changes in tasks. (Gold, p. 111)

This mix of assumptions and errors can lead to sharp contrasts. To listen to an IBM spokesman, the cost of computing has fallen very dramatically, yet for others "you can see the computer age everywhere except in the productivity statistics" (Solow). A major part of the problem is that accounting procedures seldom seek to isolate the costs of information activities. These have to include the human and organizational costs of coping with those roadblocks I mentioned earlier.

The tendency is to focus on a key feature, such as the cost of computing narrowly conceived in IBM fashion, or the cost of copying, or the cost of storage. It is easy to move from such persuasive calculations to a technological utopia such as the open network. The ultimate open network is, I suppose, cyberspace–so long as we could get rid of the sweatshops and ensure the equitable access of a society in which there were neither information rich nor information poor. But we already have a global network–the telecommunications system. I am unsure of the figure but assume it is of the order of 650 million telephones or one for every six persons; and as I mentioned earlier there are telephone rich and telephone poor. I attended a North East Asian Round Table on economic integration issues last year and had opportunity to talk with the Mongolian representative in Seoul, South Korea. He was North Korean-trained and, I believe, anxious to communicate with the participants from other North East Asian countries. He did not appear to be very successful and I was left wondering how much the average Australian would have to say to the average Mongolian. Come to think of it, what does the average social science researcher have to say to the average natural science researcher? Being active in interdisciplinary studies of the role of information, I have been particularly interested in the absence of communication between these two 'factions.' Quite often I seem to be serving as the communication link between researchers in the same institution!

Scientific journals are part of a knowledge network created to facilitate a learning process. The most basic condition is uncertainty and the participants both compete and cooperate. Human and organizational networks, in contrast to those of wire, fibre and plastic, "are an intermediate form of organization between hierarchies (internal organization within entities such as firms) and markets. Their essential function is the exchange of information. Other resources may be transferred as well, but the more commodity-like the physical resources being transferred are, the more efficient is the market mechanism. When the important resource transfer involves complex information (or know-how), the market does not function well, and other arrangements have to be made. Sometimes these arrangements involve in-house activities, e.g., when the information needs are too ill-defined and too difficult to communicate. But when the information needs become very diverse, it may be too risky and costly to try to satisfy them in-house. That is when networks become important. To put it differently, high transactions costs induce vertical integration in hierarchies, but the need to integrate is counterbalanced by the need for specialized inputs which can only be obtained from specialists. Networks make it possible to combine the advantages of vertical integration with those of specialization" (Carlsson and Stankiewicz, p. 103).

There is a harmful idea around that information is like oil, flowing easily and costlessly and improving the efficiency of the system as a whole. The reality is that information is costly; costly to produce, to transfer, and to manage. Some information activities may have been computerized while others remain labour-intensive. The open network notion might be viewed as a way of shifting costs–by operating on a do-it-yourself basis. However, the need for specialists will remain.

This brings me back to the journals. Colin Steele reminded us that the Elsevier takeover of Pergamon was valued at around one billion dollars (Australian) and yet scholars give their research free to publishers who sell it back to the universities. Some of the scholars who serve as editors suffer a further loss. My non-random sample of financial support given to editors suggests an hourly rate of pay that is even lower than that for examiners of research theses–it does not cover expenses which then have to be picked up by employing institutions or covered by outside fund raising! In a period of privatization, these matters call for attention.

I have focussed on the diffusion of knowledge aspect of journals but there are other functions that might retard the influence of the new electronic technologies. Here again I wish to suggest that an economic perspective can helpfully illuminate the theory of inquiry. Nicholas Rescher in his book *Cognitive Economy: The Economic Dimension of Knowledge* argues that treasured features of the organization of the scientific enterprise have an economic basis. The open, early exchange of information and sanctions against cheating, falsification, and carelessness are based in increased productivity.

He contends that departures from the general policy of information sharing, e.g., scientific journal secrecy practices, have "a perfectly plausible rationale in cost-benefit terms" (p. 35). According great value to priority, cooperation and team effort, and building trust all rest ultimately on economic rationality (pp. 35, 37-8, 45). The new way of providing information must not treat these time-honoured features too harshly if it is to win acceptance. And last of all a new electronic system would need to cater for needs that are just a little remote from the transfer of knowledge function: performance has to be evaluated and there have to be status symbols. These, like market transactions, call for property rights. Few have much confidence in offering information and being rewarded by a voluntary payment; collectives are in their infancy. I suspect this matter of property rights in information, especially in information that carries great potential surprise, will be the greatest roadblock—a matter that received no attention in Benedikt's *Cyberspace*.

REFERENCES

Thomas A. Bass, Review of Howard Rheingold, *I sing of cyberspace–Virtual Reality, New York Times Book Review*, 4 August 1991, p.30.

Michael Benedikt (ed.), *Cyberspace: First Steps*, MIT Press, Cambridge, Mass., 1991.

R.E. Butler, "Deregulation in the 1990s," *International Telecommunications Union*, Geneva, March 8, 1988.

B. Carlsson and R. Stankiewicz, "On the nature, function and composition of technological systems," *Evolutionary Economics*, 1, 1991, pp. 93-118.

P. Dasgupta and P.A. David, "Information disclosure and the economics of science," in G.R. Feiwel (ed.), *Arrow and the Ascent of Modern Economic Theory*, Macmillan, London, 1987, pp.519-42.

P.A. David and W.E. Steinmueller, "The impact of information technology upon economic science," *Prometheus*, 9, 1, June 1991, pp.35-61.

G. Eliasson *et al.*, *The Knowledge Based Information Economy*, Industrial Institute for Economic and Social Research, Stockholm, 1990.

Bela Gold, "On the adoption of technological innovations in industry: superficial models and complex decision processes," in S. Macdonald, D.M. Lamberton and T. Mandeville (eds), *The Trouble with Technology*, Frances Pinter, London, 1983, pp.104-21.

Richard Jinman, "Safe 'silicon' sex is a virtual reality," *The Australian*, February 12, 1991, p.31.

Donald Lamberton, "Information and the internal organization of firms," a paper presented to the American Economic Association, New Orleans, January 1992.
Axel Leijonhufvud, "Information costs and the division of labour," *International Social Science Journal*, 41, 2, May 1989, pp.165-76.
Nicholas Rescher, *Cognitive Economy: The Economic Dimension of the Theory of Knowledge*, University of Pittsburgh Press, Pittsburgh, 1989.
John Senders, "The scientific journal of the future," reprinted in A.E. Cawkell (ed.), *Evolution of an Information Society*, Aslib, London, 1987.
Robert Solow, Review of S.S. Cohen and J. Zysman, *Manufacturing Matters: The Myth of the Post-Industrial Society*, New York Times Book Review, 12 July 1987, p.36.
Colin Steele, "An electrifying age for libraries," *The Australian*, 20 November 1991, p.23.

The Electronic Journal: The Day in Retrospect

Brian Cook

The organisers have given me the unenviable task of trying to draw together the issues raised by speakers today on the advent of the e-journal. An attempt will be made to look at what threads appeared, the questions raised by speakers and some comments will be passed regarding these.

THE PAPERS

Jolanda von Hagen set the scene, in the first instance, by raising issues associated with the author's role and her/his rewards and protection for the product produced; a vexed question indeed. She then went on to look at the rights and returns to publishers especially given that they "craft" the product and bear the investment costs for that production. Client needs for scholarly information were also canvassed particularly from an access perspective. An interesting part of Jolanda's delivery was her models on pricing, publisher activities, author requirements, delivery and library involvement.

The significance of the education of all concerned with the handling of electronic information was an outcome of Jolanda's paper. This paper raises a range of questions which libraries, scholars, publishers and others will need to address before a successful electronic delivery system will be established.

Carol Newton-Smith focused strongly on issues from a site perspective. She got "to the heart of the matter" by pointing out such advantages as ease of access to information, notification of availability, the ability to search by a range of descriptions, the use of a number of platforms for access, the ability to take copies easily into personal systems and economical storage. Carol balanced her presentation by indicating that these were things people would need to consider before just 'grabbing' for the advantages listed. Among these were the need to be clear about hard and software needs for easy access as well as the need to be computer literate if maximum advantage was to be realised. Some technical problems involved in making use of e-journals were canvassed by Carol.

Carol also dealt with issues such as how to handle the advent of the electronic journal in the library, the use of intelligent desk-top systems and how to educate clients for effective use of journals available by electronic means. Cooperation in terms of client access was also featured. This emphasizes, of course, one of the things libraries tend to do–reinvent wheels. This is, again, one opportunity for cooperation.

Anne Newell commenced her presentation by reminding us that the acceptance of technology heavily depends on how people view change. There is a history of literature on this matter and libraries could do well to use some of this in planning for wider use of the electronic journal on campus. In this respect Anne emphasised the need to know the client well and then, on this basis, to plan how best to make change and align the technology needed to make sure the information made available is what is wanted.

The prime part of Anne's paper dealt with a survey associated with formats used to deliver information to clients. The results clearly indicated that the electronic format was preferred simply because it gave quick access and an overview of what and how much information was available.

The survey highlighted the following problems that still need attention–the variety, and in some cases quality, of software packages underpinning access, the fact that simply finding, by electronic means, that information is available does not necessarily mean easy access to the full-text, locating the material requires "good" document delivery processes and the questions of equity of access and who pays need to be addressed.

These issues are not new, of course. What is required now is a renewed effort to solve the problems associated with them. The emphasis must be on client need and ease of access.

Don Lamberton's title intrigued everyone–Cyberspace Economics–but all became clear as his paper focused on very real issues.

Don reminded us in the beginning that current economic and technological thinking is ensuring that the future will be different. Based on this truism Don focused attention on a wide range of issues including the need to deal with the complex problem of how people respond to technology and its intrusion into their lives.

The actual size of the information market was raised and, of course, the issue here is how much can be diverted to support this industry. Trying to forecast trends was another of Don's topics. We were reminded that current models used to forecast trends in the information sector may not be good enough. We were also reminded of the numerous failed predictions that dot our recent history in terms of information change, acceptance of technology and so on. Doubts were cast over the cost effectiveness of the use of full-text electronic journals versus current methods used to access information. This, of course, highlighted the need for more effective ways of evaluating potential performance before embracing the electronic journal too quickly.

The economics of scholarly information presented by Tom Cochrane also focused attention on aspects of the relationship that exists and, at present, must exist between scholar, editor, publisher, supplier, libraries and their clients. Tom reminded us of the need to focus on these "stakeholders" in the process if we hope to achieve a situation where electronic scholarly publishing will be readily accepted. Tom saw the possibility that like groups of scholars might be the only ones to gain from an electronic journal approach to the distribution of scholarly information.

There was a timely reminder in this paper of the fact that Australian users of scholarly information are heavily dependent on overseas sources and suppliers. Barriers to ease of access were also raised by Tom. Maybe using a concept like equity of access is not the way to approach some of the issues raised in regards to this complex matter.

The State Library of New South Wales' experience with the electronic journal was the topic presented by Janine Schmidt. Planning for the use of journals in electronic format was seen as a key issue. The experience from the State Library was "getting it right was not easy." Again, the focus needs to be on client needs and access. Much of what has been and continues to be done in the electronic information industry does not focus on the end-user. Janine reminded us that electronic access meant that emphasis on access techniques shifted back to the user.

Janine also focused on problems experienced with the production, storage and retrieval of electronic journal information. Cost implications of the electronic product versus print retrieval as well as cost to users was overviewed. There is no doubt that a lot more work needs to be done in this area before we will be sure of the cost effectiveness of scholarly information access using electronic means.

The perspective from suppliers presented by Julie Stevens dealt with issues associated with costs, access, document delivery, customer support and cost recovery for services provided. Also raised was the perspective from which we should view electronic journal products. It was suggested that one view might be to see these journals as adding value rather than being in competition with the traditional printed methods used to access scholarly information. This, of course, adds a different perspective, but can we afford both?

As with other speakers the question of the "social barriers" to technology and technological access was raised during the presentation of this paper.

THREADS THAT EMERGED

As this seminar unfolded it became obvious that a lot was happening in terms of the development of electronic scholarly publication. As a consequence a range of ideas and possibilities were placed before us that needed considered thought and addressing if all parties concerned were to maximise possibilities.

A significant thread that emerged at several times during the seminar was related to the need for continued and improved communication between authors, publishers, information technology specialists, libraries and users. These are the stakeholders in the development of the electronic journal. In simplistic terms for success and easy cooperation between such diverse groups, standardisation of formats and delivery systems seems essential. Within this framework another issue that emerged several times was the need for improved user-friendly access to information and interfaces that would ensure maximum effective access and usage of material available. For success here, users need education programs that are tailor-made to meet different access requirements.

The implications of cost of the effective input, monitoring, storage, access and protection of information that is and will be available via the electronic journal was raised. In many instances libraries are now more concerned with cost-effective services than ever before. Discussions on such topics as value-added services, questions about the legitimacy of continuing such-and-such a service at such-and-such a level are now fairly common features of managerial discussions concerning the delivery of information services.

The issue of property rights is one that has not been resolved in the electronic age. It was a feature of a number of papers presented. Coordination of effort is essential in order that we maximise the end-user's access requirements against reasonable protection for the intellectual effort of the scholarly writer. The question of achieving maximum returns is not easy, or course, when one of the principal motives of some of the players in the equation is profit. This later motive is natural given the outlay to establish effective scholarly communication by electronic means.

Cost considerations were raised by a number of people at the seminar.

Two considerations in the development of the electronic journal and other similar developments are who controls the information involved and how it will flow. In many respects Australian players in this equation are behind the "eight-ball." Many of the decisions about what constitutes scholarly information, how it will be presented, to whom, by whom, how it will be published, distributed and by what means is made overseas. There is little, if any, influence from this "isolated" region. If we want influence we will need to become involved and begin to lobby to attain it.

The issue of standards for information delivery was raised. Those of us involved with large amounts of electronically delivered information coming from numerous sources are well aware of the issues involved here. This issue must be taken away from the technical bureaucrats and placed in hands that are more conscious of user issues, chief amongst these, of course, being ease of access.

The advent of electronic information delivery has brought with it many issues to be resolved. The electronic journal is no different. In reality, developments in the delivery of scholarly information by electronic means will accelerate. We need to face this fact, address the issues and systematically resolve them for maximum user benefit. If we don't grasp this moment to resolve those things that impede a user-friendly access system then, as in the past, we will end up with a range of standards and access options controlled by a few where profit might become one of the principal driving forces.

Electronic access to information is a reality, and becoming more and more commonplace. What electronic access offers is wider access from stations no longer tied to the storage location. The problems to be faced in ensuring a delivery system that offers users wide access have been canvassed at this seminar. We have the chance to influence the outcome. Cooperative effort is now required. What should drive that is the realisation that once we put a user-friendly system in place the current technology can deliver the scholarly information available comparatively cheaply, while allowing the user to interact with that information in new and more flexible ways.

For Product Safety Concerns and Information please contact our EU representative GPSR@taylorandfrancis.com
Taylor & Francis Verlag GmbH, Kaufingerstraße 24, 80331 München, Germany

www.ingramcontent.com/pod-product-compliance
Lightning Source LLC
Chambersburg PA
CBHW052133300426
44116CB00010B/1889